COOKING FOR
ONE OR TWO

COOKING FOR ONE OR TWO

Grange
BOOKS

Published by Grange Books
An imprint of Books & Toys Limited
The Grange
Grange Yard
London SE1 3AG
By arrangement with Ebury Press

ISBN 1 85627 171 4

Consultant editor: Jeni Wright
Editors: Veronica Sperling and Barbara Croxford
Design: Mike Leaman
Illustrations: John Woodcock and Kate Simunek
Photography: David Johnson
Cookery: Susanna Tee, Maxine Clark, Janet Smith

Filmset by Advanced Filmsetters (Glasgow) Ltd

Printed and bound in Italy by
New Interlitho, S.p.a., Milan

CONTENTS

INTRODUCTION	7
SOUPS AND STARTERS	8
SUPERQUICK SNACKS	28
EVERYDAY MEALS	48
SPECIAL OCCASIONS FOR TWO	74
VEGETABLES AND SALADS	94
DESSERTS AND BAKING	108

USEFUL INFORMATION AND BASIC RECIPES

EQUIPMENT AND GADGETS	130
HEALTHY EATING	136
INGREDIENTS	140
STORAGE OF FRESH FOODS	142
USING THE FREEZER	144
LEFTOVERS	148
BASIC RECIPES	150
INDEX	159

COOKERY NOTES

Follow either metric or imperial measures for the recipes in this book as they are not inter-changeable. Sets of spoon measures are available in both metric and imperial size to give accurate measurement of small quantities. All spoon measures are level unless otherwise stated. When measuring milk we have used the exact conversion of 568 ml (1 pint).

* Size 4 eggs should be used except when otherwise stated.
† Granulated sugar is used un-less otherwise stated.
● Plain flour is used unless otherwise stated.

OVEN TEMPERATURE CHART

°C	°F	Gas mark
110	225	$\frac{1}{4}$
130	250	$\frac{1}{2}$
140	275	1
150	300	2
170	325	3
180	350	4
190	375	5
200	400	6
220	425	7
230	450	8
240	475	9

METRIC CONVERSION SCALE

LIQUID			SOLID		
Imperial	Exact conversion	Recommended ml	Imperial	Exact conversion	Recommended g
$\frac{1}{4}$ pint	142 ml	150 ml	1 oz	28.35 g	25 g
$\frac{1}{2}$ pint	284 ml	300 ml	2 oz	56.7 g	50 g
1 pint	568 ml	600 ml	4 oz	113.4 g	100 g
$1\frac{1}{2}$ pints	851 ml	900 ml	8 oz	226.8 g	225 g
$1\frac{3}{4}$ pints	992 ml	1 litre	12 oz	340.2 g	350 g
For quantities of $1\frac{3}{4}$ pints and over,			14 oz	397.0 g	400 g
litres and fractions of a litre have			16 oz (1 lb)	453.6 g	450 g
been used.			1 kilogram (kg) equals 2.2 lb.		

KEY TO SYMBOLS

1.00* Indicates minimum preparation and cooking times in hours and minutes. They do not include prepared items in the list of ingredients; calcu-lated times apply only to the method. An asterisk * indicates extra time should be allowed, so check the note below symbols.

▯ Chef's hats indicate degree of difficulty of a recipe: no hat means it is straightforward; one hat slightly more complicated; two hats indicates that it is for more advanced cooks.

£ Indicates a recipe which is good value for money; £ £ indicates an expensive recipe. No £ sign indicates an inexpensive recipe.

✳ Indicates that a recipe will freeze. If there is no symbol, the recipe is unsuitable for freezing. An asterisk * indicates special freezer instructions so check the note immediately below the symbols.

309 cals Indicates calories per serving, including any sugges-tions (e.g. cream, to serve) given in the ingredients.

COOKING FOR ONE OR TWO

If you live on your own or often eat alone, or if there are just two of you in the family, this is the cookery book you have been waiting for. No longer will you have to waste time adjusting quantities in recipes that serve four or more—all the recipes in this book have been devised with small numbers in mind.

The majority of recipes give quantities for one person, with notes on how to increase ingredients if you are serving two. All kinds of different occasions are catered for. Simple soups, starters, snacks, everyday meals and vegetable dishes, plus special occasion cookery and a welcome chapter on desserts and baking—treats that no-one should be denied! Each recipe has a full-colour photograph, and there are helpful illustrations to guide you through methods, plus menu suggestions and handy hints and tips.

In the tinted section at the back of the book there is advice on the most suitable equipment to buy, how to maintain a healthy diet and the best ingredients for one or two people, together with information on storage, using the freezer wisely and what to do with leftovers. And at the very end of the book you will find an invaluable collection of basic recipes, all of which have been scaled down to suit small needs.

Soups and Starters

Don't be tempted to do without a soup or starter when you are eating alone, or if there are just two of you sitting down to a meal. In this chapter you will find quick, no-fuss recipes that will give any meal a sense of occasion.

CRAB NOODLE SOUP

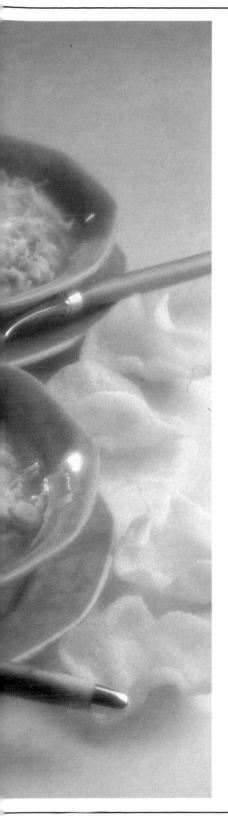

0.15 | £ | 115 cals

Serves 2

25 g (1 oz) transparent or
   cellophane noodles

80 g (3 oz) can crabmeat, drained

1 egg white, beaten

5 ml (1 tsp) sesame oil (optional)

15 ml (1 tbsp) dry sherry

5 ml (1 tsp) cornflour

2.5 ml ($\frac{1}{2}$ tsp) salt

2.5 ml ($\frac{1}{2}$ tsp) caster sugar

1 cm ($\frac{1}{2}$ inch) piece fresh root
   ginger, peeled and finely
   chopped

450 ml ($\frac{3}{4}$ pint) homemade chicken
   stock

2 spring onions, trimmed and
   finely sliced (optional)

1 Soak the noodles in boiling
water for 5 minutes. Mix the
crabmeat with the egg white and
set aside.

2 In a small bowl, mix together
the sesame oil, sherry,
cornflour, salt, sugar and ginger.

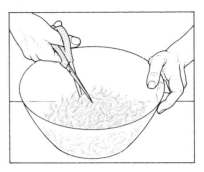

3 Drain the noodles thoroughly.
Using kitchen scissors, snip
into 2.5 cm (1 inch) lengths.

4 Bring the chicken stock to the
boil in a medium saucepan,
quickly stir in the crab and egg
white mixture, then the sherry and
cornflour mixture.

5 Bring to the boil, stirring
continuously, then add the
noodles and spring onions, if liked.
Heat through and serve
immediately.

Menu Suggestion
Serve with sake (Chinese rice
wine) and crisply fried prawn
crackers, if liked.

CRAB NOODLE SOUP

Look for Chinese transparent or
cellophane noodles in oriental
specialist shops. They are made
from ground mung beans and are
sold dried, in bundles,
sometimes also labelled 'bean
thread noodles'. In oriental
cooking, they are not served on
their own like wheat flour
noodles, but are used in soups
and other dishes which contain
liquid. They must always be
soaked in boiling water for
5 minutes before use, although
sometimes they are used as a
garnish, in which case they are
deep-fried in hot oil straight
from the packet. Cooked this way
they are crisp and crunchy—and
absolutely delicious.

   Sesame oil is made from
sesame seeds; it is a dark golden
brown in colour and thicker than
most other oils. It is used in
Chinese cooking as a flavouring
rather than for cooking, and is
well worth adding to this soup to
give it an authentic 'nutty'
flavour. Sesame oil is available in
small bottles at most large
supermarkets and oriental stores.

HOT AND SOUR SOUP

0.15*	210 cals

* plus 20 minutes soaking mushrooms

Serves 2

2 Chinese dried mushrooms, soaked

50 g (2 oz) cooked leftover meat (e.g. pork, chicken, beef or lamb)

450 ml (¾ pint) chicken stock

100 g (4 oz) tofu (see box)

30 ml (2 tbsp) cider vinegar

30 ml (2 tbsp) soy sauce

2 eggs

5 ml (1 tsp) chilli oil, or to taste (see box)

salt

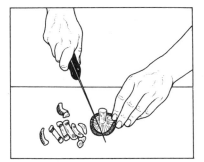

1 Drain the mushrooms, then slice very thinly. Slice the leftover meat very thinly.

2 Pour the stock into a saucepan and bring to the boil. Add the mushrooms and meat and simmer for 5 minutes.

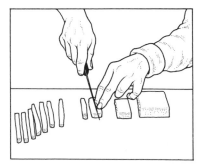

3 Meanwhile, drain the tofu and pat dry. Cut into thin strips. Add to the pan with the vinegar and soy sauce. Heat gently.

4 Crack the eggs into a bowl and add chilli oil, to taste. Beat well. Pour into the hot soup in a thin, steady stream, then stir vigorously with a fork until the eggs form threads. Taste and add salt, then pour into warmed soup bowls. Serve immediately.

Menu Suggestion

In China, soup is eaten throughout the meal rather than being served as a first course. This does not appeal to everyone in the West, however, and for this reason it is probably best to serve Chinese soups before a main course. Hot and Sour Soup goes especially well before Peking Duck (page 89).

HOT AND SOUR SOUP

Tofu, also called bean curd because it is made from soya beans, is used extensively in oriental cooking for its nutritional value — it has a very high protein content. There are two types available from health food shops and oriental stores. Silken tofu, the Japanese variety, is soft, whereas the Chinese bean curd (called *doufu*) is firm and sold in cakes or blocks. Both varieties are suitable for this soup.

Hot chilli oil can be bought in bottles from oriental stores, but it can also be made quickly and easily at home. Fry chopped dried red chillies in hot corn oil, leave to steep for 2 days, then strain into a jar with a screw-topped lid. Stored in the refrigerator, it will keep indefinitely.

ASPARAGUS SOUP

| 0.30 | £ | 240 cals |

Serves 2

1 medium potato, peeled and diced

450 ml ($\frac{3}{4}$ pint) chicken stock

275 g (10 oz) can asparagus, drained

150 ml ($\frac{1}{4}$ pint) milk

salt and freshly ground pepper

30 ml (2 tbsp) soured cream

25 g (1 oz) Gruyère cheese, grated

1 Put the diced potato and stock into a medium saucepan and bring to the boil. Simmer gently for 10–15 minutes until the potato is cooked.

2 Pour this mixture into a blender or food processor, add the drained asparagus and purée until smooth. Return to the saucepan, stir in the milk and reheat the soup thoroughly. Taste and season with salt and pepper.

3 Just before serving, stir in the soured cream and grated Gruyère cheese. Serve hot.

Menu Suggestion
Serve with warm crusty bread for an informal supper for two.

ASPARAGUS SOUP

For a special occasion, why not top this soup with a special garnish? Sprinkle grated Gruyère cheese on to buttered toast, then pop under the grill until melted and bubbling. Cut into small squares, removing the crusts, then float on top of the soup just before serving.

HAM CHOWDER

| 0.35 | ✳* | 778 cals |

* freeze without the cheese topping

Serves 2

25 g (1 oz) butter or margarine

15 ml (1 tbsp) vegetable oil

1 small onion, skinned and roughly chopped

2 celery sticks, trimmed and roughly chopped

225 g (8 oz) old potatoes, peeled and diced

300 ml ($\frac{1}{2}$ pint) milk

150 ml ($\frac{1}{4}$ pint) vegetable stock or water

2.5 ml ($\frac{1}{2}$ tsp) dried mixed herbs

salt and freshly ground pepper

175 g (6 oz) honey roast ham, diced

300 g (11 oz) can sweetcorn, drained

1 small green or red pepper, cored, seeded and roughly chopped

75 g (3 oz) Cheddar cheese, grated

1 Heat the butter with the oil in a heavy-based saucepan. Add the onion and celery and fry gently for about 5 minutes until soft but not coloured.

2 Add the potatoes and fry for a further few minutes, tossing to mix them with the onion and celery. Pour in the milk and stock and bring to the boil, stirring.

3 Add the herbs and salt and pepper to taste, then lower the heat, cover and simmer for about 20 minutes, until the potatoes are tender.

4 Add the ham, sweetcorn and pepper and cook for a further 5 minutes until heated through.

5 Pour the chowder into individual flameproof bowls. Sprinkle with the cheese, then flash under a preheated moderate grill until golden and bubbling. Serve hot.

Menu Suggestion
Chowders are always substantial soups, and this one is no exception. Serve as a main meal soup for lunch or supper, with fresh wholemeal or granary baps.

CHILLED APPLE AND AVOCADO SOUP

$\boxed{0.20^*}$ ✳* $\boxed{533\text{ cals}}$

* plus 1 hour chilling; freeze the purée without cream

Serves 2

2 Golden Delicious apples
15 g ($\frac{1}{2}$ oz) butter
5 ml (1 tsp) garam masala
300 ml ($\frac{1}{2}$ pint) chilled vegetable or chicken stock
10 ml (2 tsp) lemon juice
1 ripe avocado
150 ml ($\frac{1}{4}$ pint) single cream
salt and freshly ground pepper

1 Quarter, core and peel the apples, then slice thickly. Place in a heavy-based saucepan with the butter and garam masala. Cook, stirring, for about 5 minutes, until the apples are tender.

2 Transfer the contents of the pan to a blender or food processor. Add the stock and lemon juice and work the ingredients to a smooth purée.

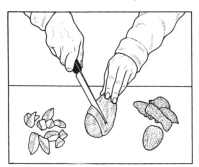

3 Peel and stone the avocado. Dice the flesh roughly with a stainless steel knife, then add to the apple mixture. Work again until smooth.

4 Pour the soup into a chilled bowl and stir in half of the cream. Add salt and pepper to taste. Cover the bowl tightly with cling film, then chill in the refrigerator for 1 hour.

5 To serve. Pour the soup into individual bowls and swirl with the remaining cream. Serve immediately, or the avocado may discolour.

Menu Suggestion
This chilled soup is cool and delicate. Serve with Melba toast for a refreshing starter in hot summer weather.

CHILLED APPLE AND AVOCADO SOUP

Garam masala is a mixture of ground spices, used frequently in Indian cooking. You can buy it in drums at most supermarkets or in Indian food shops, but it will have a fresher flavour if you make it yourself at home. Put the seeds of 4 black or 10 green cardamoms in a mortar and pestle or electric spice grinder with 15 ml (1 tbsp) black peppercorns and 10 ml (2 tsp) cumin seeds. Grind to a fine powder. Store in a screw-topped jar and use within 1 month.

MOULES MARINIÈRE

| 0.40 | £ | 685 cals |

Serves 1

600 ml (1 pint) fresh mussels

25 g (1 oz) butter or margarine

1 shallot, skinned and finely chopped

½ garlic clove, skinned and crushed

75 ml (5 tbsp) dry white wine

salt and freshly ground pepper

45 ml (3 tbsp) double cream

15 ml (1 tbsp) chopped fresh parsley

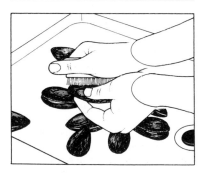

1 Put the mussels in the sink. Scrub them with a hard brush in several changes of cold water until they are clean.

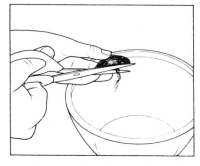

2 Scrape off any barnacles with a sharp knife. With kitchen scissors, cut off the beards or tufts of hair which may protrude from the shell.

3 Leave the mussels to soak in a bowl of cold water for 20 minutes, then discard any that are not tightly closed or do not close on giving a sharp tap. This is an important part of the preparation — any mussel that remains open is not alive and should not be cooked.

4 Melt the butter in a medium saucepan, add the shallot and fry gently until lightly coloured. Add the mussels, garlic, wine, a little salt and plenty of pepper.

5 Cover, bring to the boil and cook for 3–5 minutes until the mussels open, shaking the pan frequently.

6 Pour off the cooking juices into a small pan and add the cream. Boil rapidly until slightly thickened, then stir in the parsley.

7 Place the mussels in a soup bowl, discarding any that have not opened. Pour the sauce over the mussels and serve immediately.

8 To serve two: double the quantity of ingredients and follow the recipe above.

Menu Suggestion
Serve with crusty French bread to mop up the juices. A chilled French dry white wine such as a Muscadet goes very well.

SMOKED SALMON AND CREAM CHEESE PÂTÉ

| 0.30* | £ £ | ✳* | 473 cals |

* plus at least 2 hours chilling; freeze without the garnish

Serves 2

75 g (3 oz) smoked salmon

100 g (4 oz) full-fat soft cheese

50 g (2 oz) unsalted butter, melted and cooled

juice of $\frac{1}{2}$ lemon, or to taste

1.25 ml ($\frac{1}{4}$ tsp) cayenne pepper

2 lemon slices

10 ml (2 tsp) black lumpfish roe

1 Cut the salmon into small pieces. Place in a blender or food processor with the cheese, melted butter, juice of $\frac{1}{2}$ lemon and the cayenne pepper.

2 Work the ingredients until well mixed, then taste and add more lemon juice if liked. Spoon into 2 individual soufflé dishes or ramekins. Level the surface, cover with cling film and chill in the refrigerator for at least 2 hours.

3 To serve. Make a cut in each slice of lemon from the rind to the centre, then turn in opposite directions to make a twist.

4 Unwrap the pâtés and top each one with a twist of lemon and 5 ml (1 tsp) lumpfish roe. Serve chilled. This pâté will keep for at least 1 week in the refrigerator. Wrap tightly in cling film before storing.

Menu Suggestion
Serve with Melba toast for a special occasion starter. A chilled dry white sparkling wine would make the ideal drink.

SMOKED SALMON AND CREAM CHEESE PÂTÉ

It is not essential to buy the beautifully cut thin slivers of smoked salmon to make this pâté, because the salmon is chopped up into tiny pieces in the blender or food processor. Ask at your local delicatessen whether they sell 'off-cuts', which are the end pieces of the salmon, sometimes sold at a cheaper price than the perfect slices. Some supermarkets sell smoked salmon trout, which is also less expensive than real smoked salmon.

MARINATED KIPPER FILLETS

0.15* £ 563 cals

* plus 2–3 hours marinating

Serves 2

100 g (4 oz) kipper fillets, skinned

60 ml (4 tbsp) vegetable oil

30 ml (2 tbsp) lemon juice

15 ml (1 tbsp) chopped fresh parsley

25 g (1 oz) hazelnuts, finely chopped

1.25 ml ($\frac{1}{4}$ tsp) caster sugar

salt and freshly ground pepper

1 orange

2 spring onions, trimmed and finely sliced

shredded lettuce, to serve

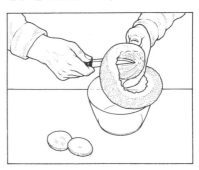

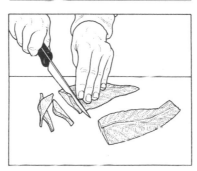

1 Cut the kipper fillets into thin strips and place in a shallow serving dish.

2 Whisk together the oil, lemon juice, parsley, hazelnuts and sugar. Season well with salt and freshly ground pepper.

3 Pour the marinade over the strips of kipper and mix well to coat evenly. Cover and leave to marinate in the refrigerator for 2–3 hours.

4 Using a sharp serrated knife, cut the top and bottom off the orange. Remove the skin by working around the orange in a spiral.

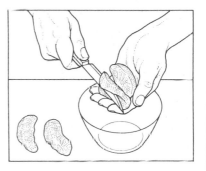

5 Divide the orange into segments by cutting either side of the membranes of each segment with a sharp knife.

6 To serve, uncover the kipper fillets and stir in the orange segments and spring onions. Line 2 plates with the shredded lettuce and pile the kipper mixture on top. Serve chilled.

Menu Suggestion

Serve the kipper fillets on their own for a starter. With crusty French bread and butter, they would make a tasty light lunch.

TAGLIATELLE WITH ANCHOVIES

| 0.15 | f | 620 cals |

Serves 1

75 g (3 oz) dried or fresh green tagliatelle

salt and freshly ground pepper

half a 50 g (2 oz) can anchovy fillets, with oil

75 ml (5 tbsp) whipping cream

30 ml (2 tbsp) chopped fresh parsley

1 Cook the tagliatelle in a medium pan of boiling salted water for 8–12 minutes if using dried, 2–3 minutes if using fresh.

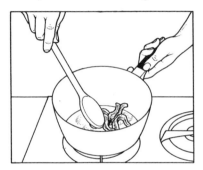

2 Meanwhile, put the anchovies with their oil into a small saucepan and cook over very low heat, crushing the anchovies with the back of a spoon until they dissolve to a purée.

3 Add the cream and increase the heat to high. Cook, stirring, for 2–3 minutes until the sauce thickens slightly. Stir in the parsley and salt and freshly ground pepper to taste.

4 Drain the tagliatelle well and add to the anchovy sauce, tossing to coat the pasta. Serve immediately.

5 To serve two: double the quantity of ingredients and follow the recipe above.

Menu Suggestion
Serve accompanied by a bowl of freshly grated Parmesan cheese, if liked. A chilled Italian dry white wine such as Frascati would go very well with the pasta and anchovy sauce.

TAGLIATELLE WITH ANCHOVIES

Tagliatelle are the flat ribbon noodles which came originally from northern Italy. They are widely available, both fresh and dried, from most large supermarkets and Italian delicatessens. Try to get the fresh variety for this recipe if possible—you will notice an enormous difference in both flavour and texture between fresh and dried. The best tagliatelle to buy is the one made with egg, labelled *all'uovo* in Italian. If you prefer a spinach flavour, buy *tagliatelle verdi*, which is often sold coiled into nests (*a nidi*). Two other types of tagliatelle which often cause confusion because they have different names, are *fettuccine*, which is simply the Roman word for tagliatelle, and *paglia e fieno*, which are nests of white and green tagliatelle or fettuccine packed together.

STUFFED GLOBE ARTICHOKE

1.25	🍴	£	713 cals

Serves 1

1 medium globe artichoke

salt and freshly ground pepper

50 g (2 oz) butter or margarine

1 small onion, skinned and finely
   chopped

50 g (2 oz) streaky bacon, rinded
   and chopped

1 medium tomato, skinned and
   roughly chopped

30 ml (2 tbsp) fresh breadcrumbs

finely grated rind and juice of
   $\frac{1}{2}$ orange

$\frac{1}{2}$ egg, beaten

15 ml (1 tbsp) chopped fresh
   parsley

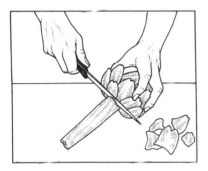

1 Cut off the stalk from the
artichoke to make a level base,
and pull off any tough or
discoloured outer leaves.

2 Trim off the tips of the
remaining artichoke leaves
with sharp kitchen scissors.

3 Place the artichoke in a pan of
boiling salted water. Cover and
boil gently for 30–40 minutes
depending on size. The artichoke
will float, so turn it during cooking
and keep covered to steam the
leaves above the water.

4 Meanwhile, make the stuffing.
Melt 25 g (1 oz) of the butter in
a saucepan, add the onion and
cook gently for 5 minutes until soft
but not coloured. Add the bacon
and cook over high heat for
1–2 minutes until golden brown.

5 Add the tomato to the pan and
cook for 2–3 minutes until
beginning to disintegrate. Stir in
the breadcrumbs, orange rind,
beaten egg, parsley and salt and
pepper to taste. Mix well.

6 Test whether the artichoke is
cooked: gently pull an outer
leaf, if it is cooked, it will come
away easily.

7 Drain the artichoke upside
down in a colander and hold
briefly under cold running water.
This helps to set the colour and
cools the leaves slightly before
handling.

8 Gradually peel back the leaves,
working from the outside
inwards (be careful not to snap any
off). Continue peeling back the
leaves until the hairy choke of the
artichoke is exposed. With a
teaspoon, scrape away and discard
the hairs.

9 Spoon the stuffing into the
cavity and gently push the
leaves back around the stuffing.
Tie string around the artichoke to
hold it together.

10 Place the artichoke in a
buttered ovenproof dish
and pour over the strained orange
juice. Cover tightly with buttered
foil and bake in the oven at 190°C
(375°F) mark 5 for 25 minutes.

11 To serve, remove the string
and place the artichoke on
an individual plate. Serve hot
accompanied by the remaining
melted butter.

12 To serve two: double the
quantity of ingredients and
follow the recipe above.

Menu Suggestion
Serve with melted butter, fingers
of wholemeal bread and a glass of
chilled dry white wine.

CARROT AND CELERIAC VINAIGRETTE

0.15* £ 410 cals

*plus 1 hour chilling

Serves 1

30 ml (2 tbsp) olive or vegetable oil, or 15 ml (1 tbsp) walnut oil and 15 ml (1 tbsp) vegetable oil, mixed

15 ml (1 tbsp) wine or cider vinegar or lemon juice

5 ml (1 tsp) wholegrain mustard

pinch of caster sugar

salt and freshly ground pepper

50 g (2 oz) celeriac

1 medium carrot

6 walnut halves, chopped

watercress sprigs or lettuce leaves, to garnish

1 Put the oil, vinegar, mustard and sugar in a small bowl. Whisk together until thick, then add salt and pepper to taste.

2 Peel the celeriac and grate into the bowl of dressing. Peel the carrot and add to the celeriac. Add the chopped walnuts and mix together thoroughly. Cover the bowl tightly with cling film. Chill in the refrigerator for at least 1 hour.

3 To serve, uncover and mix once more. Pile on to an individual serving plate and garnish with sprigs of watercress or lettuce leaves, if liked.

4 To serve two: use double the quantity of carrot, celeriac and walnuts, but use 45 ml (3 tbsp) oil and 15 ml (1 tbsp) vinegar and the same amount of sugar and mustard.

Menu Suggestion
Serve this colourful starter in winter, when both carrots and celeriac are plentiful. Granary or wholemeal bread and butter would be the ideal accompaniment.

TAPÉNADE

0.10* £ £ | 338 cals

* plus 30 minutes chilling

Serves 2

175 g (6 oz) black olives, stoned

2 anchovy fillets

1 small garlic clove, skinned and crushed

99 g (3½ oz) can tuna in oil

15 ml (1 tbsp) lemon juice

30 ml (2 tbsp) chopped fresh basil or 10 ml (2 tsp) dried

15 ml (1 tbsp) chopped fresh parsley

30 ml (2 tbsp) olive oil

salt and freshly ground pepper

1 Place all the ingredients, including the tuna oil, in a blender or food processor and work until smooth. Taste and adjust seasoning.

2 Transfer to a small bowl or 2 ramekins, cover with cling film and chill in the refrigerator for at least 30 minutes.
 Tapénade will keep in the refrigerator for up to 1 week.

Menu Suggestion
Serve with fingers of wholemeal toast and butter, or slices of crusty French bread.

TAPÉNADE
Tapénade is a popular appetiser in France, where it is served like a pâté and often included as part of a mixed hors d'oeuvre, pressed into a little pot. The name tapénade comes from *tapéno*, the Provençal word for capers. Authentic recipes from Provence include capers amongst their ingredients; if you would like to add them to this recipe, use 10 ml (2 tsp) and add them with the other ingredients — they will make the tapénade taste quite strong!

LETTUCE AND MUSHROOM COCOTTE

| 0.20 | £ | 355 cals |

Serves 1

15 g (½ oz) butter or margarine

50 g (2 oz) mushrooms, sliced

¼ small lettuce, finely shredded

2.5 ml (½ tsp) grated nutmeg

salt and freshly ground pepper

1 egg

15 ml (1 tbsp) single cream (optional)

15 ml (1 tbsp) fresh breadcrumbs

1 Melt the butter in a saucepan, add the mushrooms and cook gently for 2–3 minutes or until the mushrooms are soft, stir in the lettuce and cook for 1 minute until the lettuce is wilted. Add the nutmeg and plenty of salt and freshly ground pepper.

2 Spoon the lettuce and mushroom mixture into a small, shallow flameproof dish and make a well in the centre.

3 Crack the egg into the hollow and spoon over the cream, if liked. Sprinkle over the breadcrumbs.

4 Cook under a preheated moderate grill for about 10 minutes until the egg is just set. Serve immediately.

5 To serve two: double the quantity of ingredients and divide the mixture between 2 individual shallow flameproof dishes.

Menu Suggestion
Serve with fingers of buttered wholemeal toast for a starter, or with a mixed salad for a light lunch or supper.

LETTUCE AND MUSHROOM COCOTTE

Cultivated mushrooms are commonplace ingredients today, but in ancient times mushrooms were called the 'food of the gods' and the Egyptian Pharoahs believed that they had magical powers. These days, mushrooms are valued for their nutritional value; they are rich in protein, containing more than any other vegetable, and also extremely rich in vitamins B1, B2 and B6, plus the minerals potassium, phosphorus and copper. They are the perfect vegetable to serve for 1 or 2 people because they can be bought in small quantities and only take a few minutes to prepare and cook. Never wash cultivated mushrooms; they are grown in sterilized compost and only need wiping with a damp cloth to remove any dark spore dust.

Superquick Snacks

There are many occasions when there simply isn't time for a full-scale meal, or you simply don't feel that hungry. It's at times like these that a quick and tasty bite to eat is exactly what you need. Making a quick snack at home will ensure it is fresh and nutritious.

EGG BENEDICT

| 0.20 | 🍴 🍴 | 565 cals |

Serves 1

1 rasher streaky bacon
1 muffin
1 egg
butter or margarine, for spreading
½ quantity Hollandaise Sauce
  (page 152)
paprika and a sprig of parsley, to
  garnish

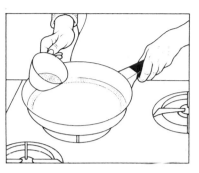

1 Cut the bacon rasher in half
  and snip off the rind with
kitchen scissors. Grill until crisp,
turning once.

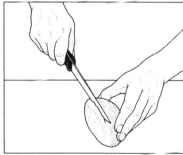

2 Cut a thin slice off the top of
  the muffin and discard. Grill
the muffin until toasted golden on
both sides.

3 Meanwhile, poach the egg
  until cooked to your liking.
Spread the muffin with butter or
margarine, then top with the
bacon and poached egg. Pour over
the hot Hollandaise Sauce, sprinkle
with paprika, garnish with the
parsley sprig and serve
immediately.

4 To serve two: cut the muffin in
  half and toast both sides. Grill
2 rashers of bacon and poach 2
eggs. Serve with 150 ml (¼ pint)
Hollandaise Sauce.

Menu Suggestion
Egg Benedict makes a superb
Sunday brunch. Serve with chilled
orange juice or orange juice and
Champagne, and extra bacon, if
liked.

EGG BENEDICT
Egg Benedict is a very popular
brunch dish in America, where it
is often served with Champagne
or Champagne cocktails —
especially on Sundays. The dish
is said to have got its name from
a certain Mr Benedict, who was
served it by a chef in a New York
restaurant as a cure for a bad
hangover! Whether this is true or
not, there is certainly something
about this dish that has a
restorative effect, which is no
doubt why it makes such a good
weekend breakfast.

BAKED EGG WITH MUSHROOMS

| 0.25 | £ | 392 cals |

Serves 1

40 g (1½ oz) butter

75 g (3 oz) button mushrooms, finely chopped

½ small onion, skinned and finely chopped

5 ml (1 tsp) chopped fresh tarragon or 2.5 ml (½ tsp) dried

salt and freshly ground pepper

1 egg

tarragon sprigs, to garnish

1 Melt half of the butter in a small frying pan, add the mushrooms and onion and fry until golden and all the excess moisture has evaporated. Add the herb and salt and pepper to taste.

2 Spoon the mushroom mixture into a ramekin or cocotte dish and make a well in the centre.

3 Carefully break an egg into the hollow, then dot with the remaining butter.

4 Stand the ramekin in a roasting tin. Pour hot water into the tin to come halfway up the side of the ramekin.

5 Cover the roasting tin with foil and bake in the oven at 180°C (350°F) mark 4 for 12–15 minutes, or until the egg is just set. Serve at once garnished with tarragon sprigs.

6 To serve two: double the quantity of ingredients, but use 50 g (2 oz) butter. Follow the recipe above, dividing the mixture between 2 ramekins.

Menu Suggestion
Serve with fingers of hot toast and butter.

OMELETTE NIÇOISE

| 0.10 | £ | 628 cals |

Serves 1

2 eggs

salt and freshly ground pepper

25 g (1 oz) unsalted butter

1 tomato, skinned and roughly
    chopped

50 g (2 oz) French beans, cooked
    and roughly chopped

5 black olives, stoned

99 g (3½ oz) can tuna, drained and
    flaked

anchovy fillets and chopped fresh
    parsley, to garnish

1 Whisk the eggs in a jug with
30 ml (2 tbsp) water and plenty
of salt and pepper.

2 Melt the butter in a small non-
stick frying pan. When the
butter is foaming, pour in the
whisked egg mixture.

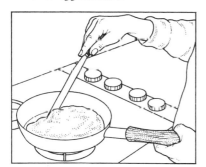

3 Cook the omelette over
moderate heat, lifting it up
around the edges with a spatula
or palette knife to allow the liquid
egg to run underneath. When the
omelette is almost set, but still
runny on top, allow the underside
to colour a little.

4 Spoon the chopped tomato,
beans, olives and tuna fish on
top of the omelette and sprinkle
with salt and pepper to taste.

5 Place the pan under a preheated
hot grill for 3–5 minutes to
heat the filling.

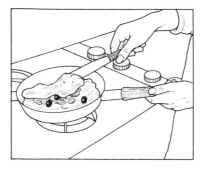

6 Fold the omelette in half,
tilting the pan away from the
handle, then turn on to a warmed
plate. Garnish with fine strips of
anchovy and chopped parsley.
Serve immediately.

7 To serve two: double the
quantity of ingredients but use
3 eggs and the same amount of
butter. Make the omelette in a
larger pan and cut the omelette in
2 before serving.

Menu Suggestion
Serve this tasty French omelette
with hot garlic or herb bread for a
substantial snack.

31

EGG AND SPINACH CROÛTE

| 0.20 | f | 798 cals |

Serves 1

2.5 cm (1 inch) thick slice of bread

50 g (2 oz) fresh spinach, washed and trimmed

65 g (2½ oz) butter

15 ml (1 tbsp) plain flour

150 ml (¼ pint) milk

freshly grated nutmeg

salt and freshly ground pepper

1 garlic clove, skinned and crushed

few drops of vinegar

1 egg

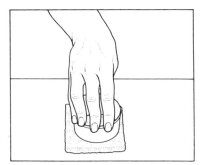

1 With a 7.5 cm (3 inch) pastry cutter, stamp out 1 round from the slice of bread. Set aside.

2 Cook the spinach with only the water that clings to the leaves for 3–4 minutes until wilted. Drain well and chop finely.

3 Melt 15 g (½ oz) of the butter in a small saucepan, add the flour and cook gently, stirring, for 1–2 minutes. Remove from the heat and gradually blend in the milk. Bring to the boil, stirring constantly, then simmer for 3 minutes until thick and smooth. Stir in the spinach and nutmeg, salt and pepper to taste. Keep hot.

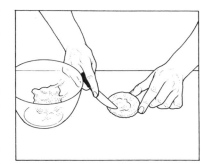

4 Toast the bread round on 1 side only. Spread the untoasted side with the remaining butter mixed with the garlic. Grill again until golden. Place the croûte on a warmed serving plate and keep hot.

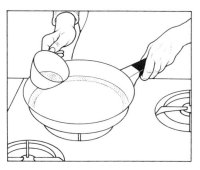

5 Half fill a frying pan with water and a few drops of vinegar. Bring the water to the boil, break the egg into a cup, then slip it into the water. Cook gently for 3–4 minutes or until lightly set, then lift out of the water with a slotted spoon.

6 Top the toasted croûte with the poached egg and spoon over the spinach. Serve immediately.

7 To serve two: double the amount of bread, spinach and eggs, but keep the remaining ingredients the same. Follow the recipe above.

Menu Suggestion
Serve Egg and Spinach Croûte on its own for a substantial and nutritious snack.

SMOKED HADDOCK SCRAMBLE

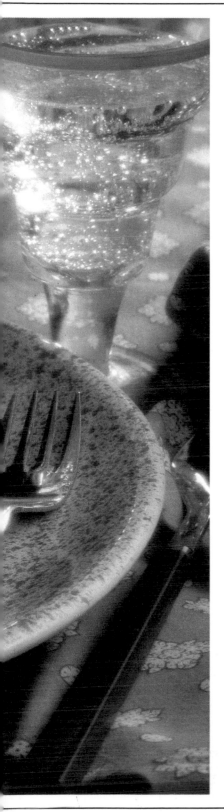

| 0.15 | £ | 705 cals |

Serves 1

2 eggs

15 ml (1 tbsp) milk

15 ml (1 tbsp) double or single
  cream

2.5 ml ($\frac{1}{2}$ tsp) lemon juice

salt and freshly ground pepper

vegetable oil, for shallow frying

1 large slice of white bread, crusts
  removed

25 g (1 oz) butter or margarine

50 g (2 oz) smoked haddock fillet,
  flaked

chopped fresh parsley, to garnish

1 In a bowl, whisk together the
eggs, milk, cream, lemon juice
and salt and pepper to taste. Set
aside while frying the bread.

2 Heat the oil in a frying pan,
add the bread and fry until
golden brown on both sides.
Remove and drain on absorbent
kitchen paper.

3 Melt the butter in a saucepan
and add the egg mixture with
the fish. Cook slowly, stirring
gently and continuously, until the
egg mixture becomes very creamy
in texture. Taste and adjust
seasoning, then remove from the
heat to prevent overcooking.

4 Place the croûte on a serving
plate, spoon over the haddock
scramble and sprinkle with
chopped parsley. Serve
immediately.

5 To serve two: double the
quantity of ingredients but use
3 eggs. Follow the recipe above.

Menu Suggestion
This dish is substantial enough to
be served on its own. Follow with
a crisp green salad tossed in
vinaigrette dressing, to refresh the
palate.

SMOKED HADDOCK SCRAMBLE

There are so many different
types of fresh and frozen smoked
fish available, both at
fishmongers and supermarkets,
that it is often difficult to know
which to choose. The best-
quality smoked haddock is the
undyed 'finnan' haddock, which
is usually sold as a whole fish,
(head removed), split open and
smoked on the bone. This type of
smoked haddock has a delicate
flavour, and is almost always
available fresh at fishmongers.
The smoked fish described as
'golden cutlets' or 'smoked white
fish fillets' are less expensive than
finnan haddock, but they may
not necessarily be haddock, and
they are often coloured with an
artificial dye. Whiting, cod and
haddock are all sold in this way;
to identify smoked haddock, look
for the 'thumb' mark on the skin
below the head.

CROQUE MONSIEUR

| 0.20 | 🍞 | 373 cals |

Serves 1

2 slices of white bread
25 g (1 oz) butter
1 slice of boiled ham
40 g (1½ oz) Gruyère cheese
salt and freshly ground pepper
15 ml (1 tbsp) vegetable oil

1 Cut the crusts off the bread, then spread 1 side of each slice with some of the butter.

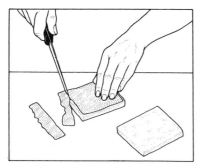

2 Place the ham on the buttered side of 1 slice of bread, cutting it to fit if necessary. Repeat with the Gruyère cheese. Sprinkle with salt and pepper to taste, then top with the remaining slice of bread, buttered side down.

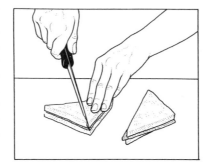

3 Press the sandwich together firmly, then cut into 4 triangles and press the edges together.

4 Melt the remaining butter with the oil in a heavy-based frying pan, add the 4 triangles and fry over moderate heat until crisp and golden on both sides. Press with a fish slice to keep the sandwiches together and turn once during frying. Serve hot.

5 To serve two: double the quantities of all the ingredients, except the oil, and follow the recipe above. If necessary, cook in 2 pans or cook in 2 separate batches.

Menu Suggestion
Toasted sandwiches are the ideal quick snack when you arrive home hungry and cannot wait to cook a proper meal. Serve with a simple mixed salad of shredded lettuce, slices of tomato and cucumber and mustard and cress.

CROQUE MONSIEUR

This tasty toasted cheese and ham sandwich is sold in bars and cafés all over France. Croque Monsieur is the classic recipe, but there is now also another version called Croque Madame, which is the same except that it is served topped with a lightly poached egg.

Gruyère is the correct cheese to use, but in France it is possible to buy packets of processed 'Croque Monsieur' cheese slices, which have been cut to shape for the sliced bread the French use when making this sandwich. Outside France, you can use any processed cheese slices or, better still, slices of Danish Samsoe or Havarti cheese, which are less expensive than Gruyère.

WELSH RAREBIT

| 0.10 | £ | 530 cals |

Serves 1

50 g (2 oz) Cheddar cheese, grated

25 g (1 oz) butter or margarine

15 ml (1 tbsp) brown ale

1.25 ml ($\frac{1}{4}$ tsp) mustard powder

salt and freshly ground pepper

1 slice of bread, crusts removed

1 Place all the ingredients except the bread in a heavy-based saucepan. Heat very gently, stirring continuously, until a creamy mixture is obtained.

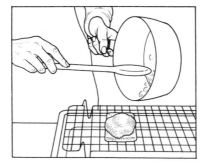

2 Lightly toast the bread on 1 side only. Pour the sauce over the uncooked side and cook under a preheated hot grill until it is golden and bubbling.

3 To serve two: use the same amount of butter, but double the other ingredients. Follow the recipe above.

Menu Suggestion
Serve for a quick evening meal with a tankard of brown ale and a colourful mixed salad.

— VARIATION —

BUCK RAREBIT
This is Welsh Rarebit topped with **a poached egg.**

FRENCH BREAD PIZZA

| 0.10 | £ | 1067 / cals |

Serves 1

50 g (2 oz) salami, sliced and
    chopped and rinded

1 large ripe tomato, skinned and
    chopped

3 black olives, stoned and sliced

50 g (2 oz) Mozzarella or Bel Paese
    cheese, grated

freshly ground pepper

½ small French loaf

50 g (2 oz) butter or margarine

15 ml (1 tbsp) snipped fresh chives
    or 5 ml (1 tsp) dried mixed herbs

1 In a bowl, combine the salami,
tomato, olives and half of the
cheese. Season with pepper.

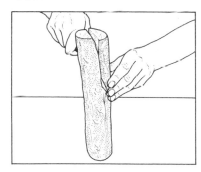

2 Trim the end off the French
bread and split in half
lengthwise. Toast both pieces on
each side.

3 Spread the toasted side
generously with the butter and
scatter the chives on top.

4 Spoon on the salami mixture,
then top with the rest of the
grated cheese. Cook under a hot
grill for 2 minutes or until the
cheese melts. Serve immediately.

5 To serve two: double the
quantity of ingredients and
follow the recipe above.

Menu Suggestion
Serve French Bread Pizza with a
crisp mixed salad tossed in an oil
and vinegar dressing.

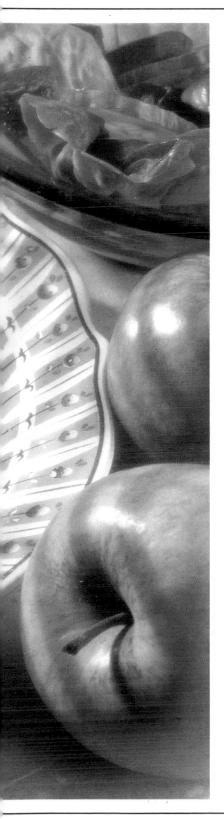

BACON, CHEESE AND APPLE SMOKIES

| 0.10 | £ | 487 cals |

Serves 1

2.5 cm (1 inch) thick slice of crusty bread

15 g ($\frac{1}{2}$ oz) butter or margarine

$\frac{1}{2}$ eating apple, cored and sliced

50 g (2 oz) smoked Applewood or Edam cheese

2 lean rashers of streaky bacon, rinded

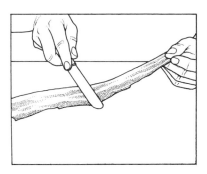

1 Toast the bread lightly on both sides, then spread 1 side with the butter. Arrange the apple slices on top of the buttered toast.

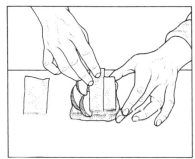

2 Slice the cheese thinly and place on top of the apple slices to cover them completely.

3 Stretch the bacon rashers with the back of a knife and cut each rasher in half. Use the bacon to cover the cheese.

4 Place the toast under a moderate grill for about 5 minutes, or until the bacon is golden and the cheese is beginning to melt. Serve immediately.

5 To serve two: double the quantity of ingredients and follow the recipe above.

Menu Suggestion
Serve this toasted snack with a salad of sliced tomatoes and raw onions dressed with olive oil, lemon juice, chopped fresh herbs and salt and pepper.

BACON, CHEESE AND APPLE SMOKIES

Applewood is an English hard cheese, a mature Cheddar which has been smoked with an outer coating of paprika. There is another similar English smoked cheese called Charwood. Both can be obtained from good supermarkets and specialist cheese shops, and they will give this tasty snack an unusual 'smoky' flavour. If you are unable to obtain them, other good smoked cheeses to look for are Smoked Emmental, which can be recognised easily by its brown plastic casing (it is made in a long sausage shape), and a similar British version called 'Bavarian Smoked Cheese'. There is also a smoked Mozzarella, an interesting-looking Italian cheese, but this is only available at specialist Italian delicatessens.

CALIFORNIAN CLUB SANDWICH

0.10	768 cals

Serves 1

3 slices of wholemeal bread
butter or margarine, for spreading
1 lettuce leaf
30 ml (2 tbsp) mayonnaise
salt and freshly ground pepper
2 slices of Swiss cheese (Gruyère or
**   Emmental)**
1 slice of canned pineapple, well
**   drained**
2 slices of cold cooked chicken,
**   skinned**
1 small tomato, sliced

1 Toast the slices of bread on both sides, removing the crusts if wished. Spread 1 side of 1 slice with butter or margarine, then cover with the lettuce leaf.

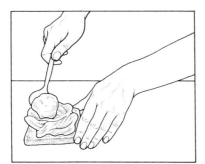

2 Spoon half of the mayonnaise on to the lettuce and sprinkle with salt and pepper to taste. Place the cheese on top, then the pineapple.

3 Spread another slice of toast on both sides with butter or margarine. Place over the pineapple, then spread with the remaining mayonnaise. Arrange the chicken and tomato slices on the mayonnaise and sprinkle with more salt and pepper to taste.

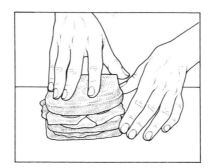

4 Spread the remaining slice of toast with butter or margarine, then place this buttered side down on top of the sandwich.

5 Cut the sandwich diagonally into quarters and secure each one with a cocktail stick. Serve immediately.

6 To serve two: double all the ingredients and follow the recipe above.

Menu Suggestion
Serve for a quick and nutritious lunchtime snack with a glass of ice-cold beer or lager.

BACON, LETTUCE AND TOMATO TOASTED SANDWICH

0.10	538 cals

Serves 1

3 rashers streaky bacon, rinded
2 slices of wholemeal or granary
**   bread, toasted**
about 30 ml (2 tbsp) mayonnaise
a few lettuce leaves
1 medium tomato, sliced
salt and freshly ground pepper

1 Fry the bacon in its own fat until crisp; drain on absorbent kitchen paper. Spread 1 side of each slice of toast with some of the mayonnaise.

2 Arrange the lettuce on 1 slice of toast, top with the tomato and sprinkle with salt and pepper.

3 Arrange the bacon over the tomato and top with the remaining toast slice, mayonnaise side down.

4 Cut the sandwich diagonally into quarters and secure each one with a cocktail stick. Arrange, crust sides down, on a plate

5 To serve two: double the quantity of ingredients and follow the recipe above.

Menu Suggestion
Serve this sandwich American-style, with ice-cold lager or beer.

BACON, LETTUCE AND TOMATO TOASTED SANDWICH
Called BLTs for short, these sandwiches originated in America, there they are served as a superquick snack at drug store counters and bars. The formula is always the same, no matter where they are made. Americans use 'tendersweet' or 'tendercure' bacon, which is mild in flavour and not at all salty.

HOT PITTA PACKET

| 0.15 | £ | 414 cals |

Serves 1

30 ml (2 tbsp) vegetable oil

1 cooked chicken leg, skinned, boned and shredded

75 g (3 oz) button mushrooms, sliced

$\frac{1}{2}$ a small red pepper, cored, seeded and finely sliced

2.5 ml ($\frac{1}{2}$ tsp) chilli seasoning

15 ml (1 tbsp) soy sauce

2.5 ml ($\frac{1}{2}$ tsp) granulated sugar

5 ml (1 tsp) sesame oil (optional)

1 medium carrot, peeled and grated

50 g (2 oz) cabbage, finely sliced

salt and freshly ground pepper

1 wholemeal pitta bread

1 Heat the oil in a frying pan, add the chicken, mushrooms, and red pepper and fry, stirring continuously, for 2–3 minutes.

2 In a jug, mix the chilli seasoning with the soy sauce, sugar, oil (if using) and salt and pepper to taste. Add to the chicken with the remaining vegetables and cook over high heat for a further 2 minutes, stirring all the time.

3 Grill the pitta bread under a moderate heat on each side for about 2 minutes.

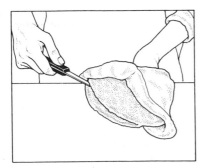

4 Using a sharp knife, make a slit along 1 edge of the pitta bread. Open the bread up carefully to form a pocket.

5 Spoon the chicken and vegetable mixture carefully into the pitta packet and serve immediately.

6 To serve two: double the quantity of ingredients and follow the recipe above.

Menu Suggestion
With its filling of chicken and vegetables, this pitta packet is substantial enough to be served on its own.

CHEESY SALAMI GRATIN

1.00 | **1272 cals**

Serves 1

2 medium potatoes

salt and freshly ground pepper

1 egg

25 g (1 oz) Parmesan cheese, grated

15 g (½ oz) butter

2 tomatoes, skinned and sliced

100 g (4 oz) Mozzarella or Gruyère cheese, sliced

50 g (2 oz) Italian salami, rinded and chopped

10 ml (2 tsp) chopped fresh basil or 5 ml (1 tsp) dried

1 Cook the potatoes in their skins in boiling salted water for about 20 minutes, or until tender.

2 Drain the potatoes and leave until cool enough to handle, then carefully peel off the skins with your fingers.

3 Mash the potatoes in a bowl then add the egg, Parmesan and salt and pepper to taste. Beat well to mix.

4 Brush the inside of an individual gratin dish with some of the butter. Spoon half of the mashed potato in the bottom of the dish. Cover with half of the tomato slices, then half of the cheese and salami.

5 Sprinkle each layer with basil and salt and pepper to taste, taking care not to add too much salt because the cheese and salami may be salty. Repeat the layers of potato, tomato, cheese and salami, sprinkling each with the remaining basil and seasoning to taste.

6 Dot with the remaining butter, then bake in the oven at 230°C (450°F) mark 8 for 15 minutes until golden brown and bubbling. Serve hot, straight from the dish.

7 To serve two: follow the recipe above, doubling the quantity of all the ingredients, but only increasing the basil by half.

Menu Suggestion
This gratin dish is very rich and filling. Serve with a crisp and colourful mixed salad.

GLAZED SPICY SAUSAGES

| 0.25 | 395 cals |

Serves 1

finely grated rind and juice of
  1 small orange
90 ml (6 tbsp) mild chilli sauce
30 ml (2 tbsp) clear honey
5 ml (1 tsp) salt
5 ml (1 tsp) Worcestershire sauce
freshly ground pepper
2 fat pork sausages

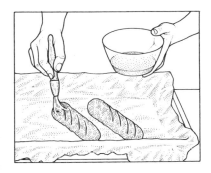

1 Make the glaze. Mix the orange rind and juice with the chilli sauce, honey, salt, Worcestershire sauce and pepper to taste. (This glaze will keep for up to 2 weeks in a screw-top jar in the refrigerator.)

3 Brush the glaze generously over the sausages. Cook the sausages under a moderate grill for 10–15 minutes or until cooked through, turning and basting occasionally with more chilli glaze. Serve immediately.

4 To serve two: double the number of sausages and use the same amount of glaze.

Menu Suggestion
Serve as 'hot dogs' in warmed long rolls or, for a more substantial meal, serve with creamed potatoes and a seasonal vegetable.

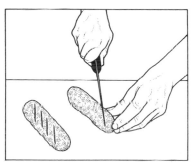

2 Slash the sausages diagonally in 4 places and place in a foil-lined grill pan.

GLAZED SPICY SAUSAGES

Chilli sauce is used extensively in Chinese food, both as a dip and in cooking; it can be bought at oriental specialist stores and some large supermarkets. It is bright red in colour, made from a mixture of hot chillies, vinegar, sugar and salt. Some brands are fiery hot, so experiment with a few different ones until you find one that suits your taste. Treat any chilli sauce with caution, however, and add sparingly at first, until you are sure of its strength! If liked, you can use Tabasco as a substitute, but in this recipe you will only need a few drops.

Everyday Main Meals

If you are living alone, everyday main meals are most important from a nutritional point of view, and a balanced diet with plenty of variety is essential. In this chapter you will find many imaginative ideas using fresh, healthy ingredients, to tempt your tastebuds from day to day.

INDIVIDUAL COTTAGE PIE

| 0.45 | £ | ✳* | 1074 cals |

* freeze at step 7, before dotting with butter and grilling

Serves 1

2 medium carrots, peeled and chopped

salt and freshly ground pepper

30 ml (2 tbsp) vegetable oil

1 small onion, skinned and finely chopped

100–175 g (4–6 oz) minced beef

275 g (10 oz) old potatoes

225 g (8 oz) can tomatoes

15 ml (1 tbsp) Worcestershire sauce

2.5 ml ($\frac{1}{2}$ tsp) dried mixed herbs

1.25 ml ($\frac{1}{4}$ tsp) mustard powder

1 egg, size 5 or 6, beaten

15 g ($\frac{1}{2}$ oz) butter or margarine

30 ml (2 tbsp) milk

1 Cook the chopped carrots in boiling salted water for 10 minutes until tender.

2 Meanwhile, heat the oil in a saucepan, add the onion and fry gently for about 5 minutes until soft but not coloured. Add the minced beef and fry over moderate heat, stirring to break up any lumps.

3 Remove the carrots from the water with a slotted spoon and set aside. Add the potatoes and cook for 20 minutes or until tender.

4 Meanwhile, add the tomatoes to the beef with their juice, the Worcestershire sauce, herbs, mustard and salt and pepper to taste. Simmer for about 20 minutes, stirring occasionally.

5 Drain the potatoes and transfer to a bowl. Mash until smooth, then add the egg, half of the butter, the milk and salt and pepper to taste. Beat well to mix.

6 Add the carrots to the minced beef mixture and heat through. Transfer the mixture to an individual gratin dish and spoon the potato on top.

7 Mark the mashed potato with a fork, then dot with the remaining butter. Put under a preheated hot grill for about 5 minutes until the potato is crisp and golden brown. Serve hot.

8 To serve two: follow the recipe above, increasing the quantity of carrots to 3, the minced beef to 225–350 g (8–12 oz) and the potatoes to 450 g (1 lb).

Menu Suggestion

Serve with a seasonal green vegetable such as Brussels sprouts sprinkled with grated nutmeg, or stir-fried shredded cabbage.

SAUTÉ OF LAMB WITH COURGETTES AND MUSHROOMS

| 0.40 | ✳ | 747 cals |

Serves 1

175 g (6 oz) boneless lamb fillet

30 ml (2 tbsp) vegetable oil

1 small onion, skinned and finely chopped

1 small garlic clove, skinned and crushed

15 ml (1 tbsp) tomato purée

300 ml (½ pint) hot chicken stock

5 ml (1 tsp) chopped fresh rosemary or 2.5 ml (½ tsp) dried

salt and freshly ground pepper

25 g (1 oz) butter or margarine

2 small courgettes, trimmed and sliced

50–75 g (2–3 oz) button mushrooms, wiped and sliced

sprig of rosemary, to garnish (optional)

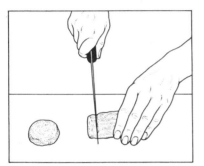

1 Cut the lamb into thin slices, discarding all fat and sinew. Heat the oil in a heavy-based frying pan, add the lamb and fry over brisk heat until well browned on all sides. Remove with a slotted spoon and drain on absorbent kitchen paper.

2 Add the onion and garlic to the pan and fry gently for about 5 minutes until soft but not coloured. Dissolve the tomato purée in the hot stock, then pour into the pan. Return the meat to the pan, then sprinkle in the rosemary and salt and pepper to taste. Simmer, uncovered, for 20 minutes until the lamb is tender.

3 Melt the butter in a separate frying pan, add the courgettes and mushrooms and toss over high heat for about 5 minutes.

4 Add the courgettes and mushrooms to the lamb, increase the heat and stir fry until most of the liquid has evaporated and the sauce just coats the meat and vegetables. Taste and adjust seasoning before serving. Garnish with a sprig of rosemary, if liked.

5 To serve two: follow the recipe above, increasing the lamb to 350 g (12 oz), the stock to 450 ml (¾ pint), the courgettes to 3 and the mushrooms to 100 g (4 oz).

Menu Suggestion

For a substantial supper, serve on a bed of boiled rice. Vegetables are included with the lamb, so no further accompaniment is necessary. A bowl of soured cream can be served separately, if wished.

SAUTÉ OF LAMB WITH COURGETTES AND MUSHROOMS

Boneless lamb fillet is an excellent, quick-cooking cut of meat to use for everyday meals; it is also good threaded on skewers for kebabs. It is cut from the neck and is inexpensive yet lean and very juicy. Ask your butcher to cut it for you, or buy it frozen from large supermarkets.

LAMB AND AUBERGINE CURRY

| 2.00 | £ £ ✳ | 421 cals |

Serves 2

450 g (1 lb) lean boneless lamb, cut
    into 2.5 cm (1 inch) cubes

15 g ($\frac{1}{2}$ oz) plain flour

30 ml (2 tbsp) vegetable oil

1 onion, skinned and sliced

1 garlic clove, skinned and crushed

15–30 ml (1–2 tbsp) curry powder

300 ml ($\frac{1}{2}$ pint) beef stock or water

30 ml (2 tbsp) tomato purée

pinch of ground cinnamon

pinch of ground cloves

salt and freshly ground pepper

1 small aubergine

parsley or coriander sprigs, to
    garnish

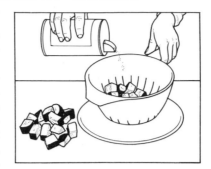

4 Meanwhile, trim the aubergine and cut into 2.5 cm (1 inch) chunks. Place in a colander, sprinkling each layer with salt. Cover with a plate, place heavy weights on top and leave to dégorge for 30 minutes.

1 Toss the lamb in the flour to coat. Heat the oil in a large frying pan, add the meat a few pieces at a time and brown on all sides, transferring the pieces to a bowl as they are browned.

2 Add the onion, garlic and curry powder to the oil remaining in the pan, and cook over low heat for about 5 minutes, stirring frequently until the onion is soft but not coloured.

3 Return the meat to the pan and stir in the stock, tomato purée, cinnamon, cloves, 5 ml (1 tsp) salt and pepper to taste. Bring to the boil, then lower the heat, cover and simmer gently for 1 hour, stirring occasionally to prevent sticking.

5 Rinse the aubergine, pat dry with absorbent kitchen paper and stir into the curry. Add a little more stock or water if necessary, cover and continue cooking for another 30 minutes, or until the aubergine is tender. Serve hot, garnished with parsley or coriander sprigs.

Menu Suggestion
Serve with plain boiled rice and side dishes such as sliced banana tossed in shredded coconut, sliced cucumber and yogurt, and mango chutney or hot lime pickle.

ROQUEFORT RUMPBURGER

| 0.30 | £ £ ✳* | 564 cals |

* freeze at the end of step 3, before grilling

Serves 1

175 g (6 oz) piece of rump steak, with surrounding fat
¼ small onion, skinned
few sprigs of fresh parsley
salt and freshly ground pepper
25–40 g (1–1½ oz) Roquefort cheese
vegetable oil, for brushing

1 Work the steak, onion and parsley through a mincer, or in a food processor. Season well with salt and pepper.

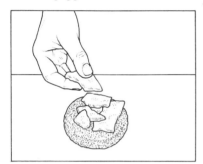

2 Place half of the meat mixture on a board and form into a flat burger shape. Cut the Roquefort in slices to fit on top of the burger.

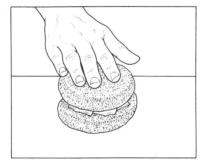

3 Form the remaining meat mixture into a burger shape and place over the cheese. Press down well and make sure that the meat covers the cheese completely.

4 Place the burger on the rack in the grill pan and brush lightly with oil. Grill under a preheated moderate grill for 3–5 minutes or until cooked to your liking.

5 Turn the burger over, brush with more oil and grill the other side for a further 3–5 minutes. Serve hot.

6 To serve two: double the quantity of all the ingredients and follow the recipe above.

Menu Suggestion
These burgers taste extra good with a tomato sauce (page 153) and a mixed salad.

CHINESE BEEF WITH MUSHROOMS AND OYSTER SAUCE

| 0.40 | £ £ | 408 cals |

Serves 2

25 g (1 oz) Chinese dried
  mushrooms

175–225 g (6–8 oz) rump steak

30 ml (2 tbsp) oyster sauce
  (see box)

30 ml (2 tbsp) dry sherry

salt and freshly ground pepper

30 ml (2 tbsp) vegetable oil

1 small onion, skinned and thinly
  sliced

1 garlic clove, skinned and crushed

2.5 cm (1 inch) piece of fresh root
  ginger, peeled

2 carrots, peeled

10 ml (2 tsp) cornflour

1 Put the dried mushrooms in a bowl, pour in boiling water to cover and leave to soak for about 20 minutes.

2 Meanwhile, cut the steak into thin strips, place in a bowl and add the oyster sauce, sherry and salt and pepper to taste. Stir well to mix, then cover and leave to marinate in a cool place while the mushrooms are soaking.

3 Heat the oil in a wok or deep, heavy-based frying pan. Add the onion and garlic and fry gently for about 5 minutes until soft but not coloured, stirring occasionally.

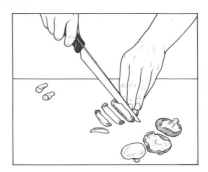

4 Meanwhile, drain the mushrooms and reserve the soaking liquid. Squeeze the mushrooms dry, then slice thinly, discarding any hard stalks. Cut into thin matchstick strips.

5 Add the mushrooms, ginger and carrots to the wok and stir fry over moderate heat for about 5 minutes until slightly softened. Add the meat and marinade and stir fry for a few minutes more, until the beef is tender.

6 Mix the cornflour to a paste with 60 ml (4 tbsp) of the soaking water from the mushrooms. Pour into the wok and stir fry until the sauce is thickened. Taste and adjust seasoning before serving.

Menu Suggestion
Serve this quick-and-easy Chinese stir fry with boiled Chinese egg noodles or rice.

CHINESE BEEF WITH MUSHROOMS AND OYSTER SAUCE

Look for packets of Chinese dried mushrooms in oriental specialist shops; they are very expensive, but are only used in small quantities because their flavour is so strong. After opening the packet, store them carefully in an airtight jar in a cool, dark place, where they will keep for many months. Chinese dried mushrooms must always be softened in warm water for 20 minutes or so before use, so be sure not to omit this important part of their preparation.

Oyster sauce, as its name suggests, is made from oysters mixed with soy sauce and brine. Sold in bottles in oriental shops, it is very thick and rich, and should be used sparingly. Once opened, store in the refrigerator.

BACON OLIVES

1.00	990 cals

Serves 1

25 g (1 oz) butter

1 small onion, skinned and finely
    chopped

50 g (2 oz) Italian risotto rice

400 ml (12 fl oz) hot chicken stock

50 g (2 oz) dried apricots, finely
    chopped

1 eating apple, cored and finely
    chopped

30 ml (2 tbsp) chopped fresh
    coriander

2.5 ml ($\frac{1}{2}$ tsp) ground cinnamon

salt and freshly ground pepper

1 thinly cut gammon rasher

300 ml ($\frac{1}{2}$ pint) dry cider

sprig of coriander, to garnish
    (optional)

1 Melt the butter in a heavy-
based saucepan, add the onion
and fry gently for about 5 minutes.

2 Add the rice and stir to coat in
the butter and onion. Add a
third of the stock and cook until the
rice is dry. Repeat with remaining
stock, cooking for 15–20 minutes.

3 Remove the pan from the heat
and add the apricots, apple,
half of the coriander, the
cinnamon and salt and pepper to
taste. (Salt sparingly, in case the
gammon is salty.) Stir well.

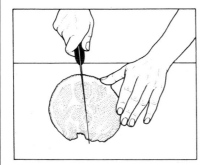

4 Cut the gammon rasher in
half, trimming off any rind and
fat. Place between 2 sheets of
dampened greaseproof paper and
bat out thinly with a rolling pin.

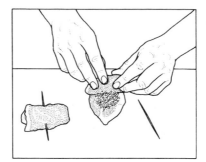

5 Divide the risotto filling
equally between the 2 pieces of
gammon, then roll the gammon up
and secure with cocktail sticks.

6 Pour the cider or stock into the
saucepan in which the risotto
was made. Bring to the boil,
stirring to scrape up any sediment.
Lower the heat, add the bacon
olives and sprinkle with pepper to
taste. Cover and simmer for
20 minutes or until the bacon feels
tender when pierced with a skewer.

7 Lift the bacon olives out of the
liquid and place on a warmed
plate. Discard the cocktail sticks.
Cover and keep hot.

8 Boil the cooking liquid to
reduce slightly, then remove
from the heat and stir in the
remaining coriander. Taste and
adjust seasoning, then pour over
the bacon olives. Serve hot,
garnished with the coriander
sprigs, if liked.

9 To serve two: double the
quantity of gammon, rice,
stock, apricots and apple and
increase the stock to 450 ml
($\frac{3}{4}$ pint), otherwise follow the
recipe above.

Menu Suggestion
Serve with extra risotto rice or
creamed potatoes, and a seasonal
vegetable such as sliced courgettes
pan-fried in butter and olive oil.

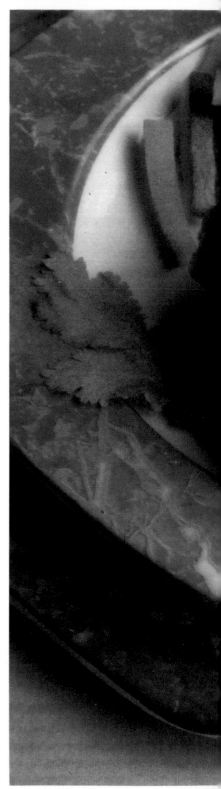

PORK BROCHETTES

0.20* £ 387 cals

* plus 1 hour marinating

Serves 1

175–225 g (6–8 oz) pork fillet
15 ml (1 tbsp) lemon juice
15 ml (1 tbsp) olive or vegetable oil
2.5 ml ($\frac{1}{2}$ tsp) paprika
1.25 ml ($\frac{1}{4}$ tsp) dried oregano
1.25 ml ($\frac{1}{4}$ tsp) cayenne
pinch of ground cumin
pinch of ground coriander
salt and freshly ground pepper
cucumber rolls, to garnish

1 Trim the pork of any fat or gristle and cut into 2 cm ($\frac{3}{4}$ inch) cubes.

2 In a medium-sized bowl, mix together the lemon juice, oil, paprika, oregano, cayenne, cumin, coriander and salt and pepper to taste. Add the cubed pork and mix well to coat. Cover and leave to marinate in the refrigerator for at least 1 hour.

3 Thread the pork cubes on to kebab skewers. Cook under a preheated hot grill for about 12 minutes, turning the brochettes occasionally to ensure even cooking. Baste occasionally with any remaining marinade. Serve immediately, garnished with the cucumber rolls.

4 To serve two: double the quantity of ingredients and use the same amount of cayenne but 1.25 ml ($\frac{1}{4}$ tsp) cumin and coriander. Follow the recipe above.

Menu Suggestion
Serve on a bed of shredded lettuce dressed with olive oil and lemon juice. A dish of plain boiled rice would go well as a contrast to the spicy pork.

PORK BROCHETTES

Pork fillet, sometimes also called tenderloin, is a very popular cut of meat because it is so lean and tender. If cut into thin slices it will literally cook in a few minutes—perfect for everyday meals when you are in a rush. This recipe marinates the pork for at least 1 hour, which, although not absolutely essential, does help to moisten the meat. All lean meats benefit from marinating if you have the time, they should also be basted during cooking because they have so little natural fat. This recipe could equally well be made with lamb fillet, or even with cubes of boneless chicken breast meat.

SPICY SAUSAGES WITH LENTILS

| 0.30 | £ | 695 cals |

Serves 1

75 g (3 oz) red lentils

15 ml (1 tbsp) vegetable oil

1 small onion, skinned and finely sliced

2 peperami sausages, thinly sliced

2.5 ml ($\frac{1}{2}$ tsp) tomato purée

1.25 ml ($\frac{1}{4}$ tsp) turmeric

10 ml (2 tsp) wholemeal or plain flour

75 ml (5 tbsp) Simple Tomato Sauce (page 153)

salt and freshly ground pepper

chopped fresh parsley, to garnish

1 Put the lentils into a pan of water. Bring to the boil and cook for about 20 minutes or until soft. Drain and reserve.

2 Heat the oil in a small frying pan, add the onion, sausage, tomato purée and turmeric and cook, stirring, for about 5 minutes.

3 Sprinkle over the flour and cook for 1 further minute. Add the lentils and tomato sauce, bring to the boil and simmer gently for about 2–3 minutes or until thickened. Taste and season with salt and pepper. Serve hot, sprinkled with chopped parsley.

4 To serve two: double the quantity of ingredients but only use 15 ml (1 tbsp) flour. Follow the recipe above.

Menu Suggestion
Serve with brown rice for a most nutritious meal, followed by a crisp green salad.

CHICKEN JAMBALAYA

| 0.45 | 816 cals |

Serves 1

30 ml (2 tbsp) vegetable oil

1 chicken portion

1 small onion, skinned and finely chopped

1 small green pepper, cored, seeded and finely chopped

2 ripe tomatoes, skinned and roughly chopped

75 g (3 oz) brown rice

1 bay leaf

10 ml (2 tsp) chopped fresh parsley or 5 ml (1 tsp) dried

5 ml (1 tsp) chopped fresh thyme or 2.5 ml ($\frac{1}{2}$ tsp) dried

1.25 ml ($\frac{1}{4}$ tsp) cayenne pepper

salt and freshly ground pepper

1 Heat the oil in a heavy-based flameproof casserole or saucepan. Add the chicken and fry until golden brown on all sides. Remove with a slotted spoon and drain on absorbent kitchen paper.

2 Add the onion, pepper and tomatoes to the pan. Fry gently for about 5 minutes, stirring until softened but not coloured. Add the rice and stir to mix with the onion, pepper and tomato.

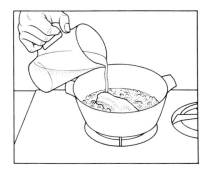

3 Return the chicken to the pan and pour in enough cold water to cover. Add the bay leaf, parsley, thyme, cayenne and salt and pepper to taste.

4 Stir well to mix and bring to the boil. Cover and simmer gently for 30 minutes, or until the chicken and rice are both tender and most of the liquid absorbed.

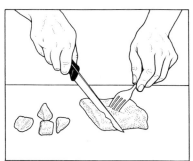

5 Lift the chicken portion out of the pan. Remove the flesh from the bone, then cut into bite-sized cubes, discarding the skin.

6 Return the chicken pieces to the pan and heat through. Season and remove the bay leaf.

7 To serve two: follow the recipe above, using 2 chicken portions, 1 medium onion, 1 medium pepper, 150 g (6 oz) brown rice and 3 tomatoes.

Menu Suggestion
Serve this tasty Creole dish with a crisp green salad.

PAN-GRILLED CHICKEN BREASTS WITH HERBS

0.35	465 cals

Serves 1

175 g (6 oz) chicken breast
25 g (1 oz) butter
15 ml (1 tbsp) olive oil
1 garlic clove, skinned and crushed
juice of ½ lemon
5 ml (1 tsp) chopped fresh tarragon
  or 2.5 ml (½ tsp) dried
5 ml (1 tsp) chopped fresh fennel or
  2.5 ml (½ tsp) dried
salt and freshly ground pepper
lemon slices and watercress
  sprigs, to garnish (optional)

1 Remove and discard the skin from the chicken breast, and the bone if necessary. Set aside.

2 Melt the butter with the oil in a small saucepan. Remove from the heat and add the garlic, lemon juice and herbs.

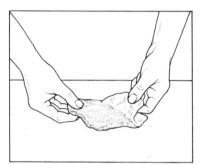

3 Brush the base of the grill pan with a little of the melted mixture. Place the chicken in the pan and brush with more mixture.

4 Put the pan under a preheated moderate grill and cook for 15–20 minutes. Turn the chicken several times during grilling and brush with more of the herb mixture. Sprinkle with salt and pepper to taste at the end of the cooking time. Serve hot, garnished with lemon slices and sprigs of watercress, if liked.

5 To serve two: follow the recipe above, doubling the quantities of all the ingredients except the herbs, which should only be increased by half.

Menu Suggestion
Serve with a jacket-baked potato, grilled tomatoes and a seasonal green vegetable.

PAN-GRILLED CHICKEN BREASTS WITH HERBS
Tarragon and chicken have a natural affinity for one another, but did you know that there are two different types of tarragon? French tarragon is the best culinary variety, with a fairly strong, spicy flavour. It is a perennial herb, which grows easily in a sheltered spot in the garden. Russian tarragon is considered inferior in cooking because it has hardly any flavour. If possible, use fresh tarragon in chicken recipes such as this one—dried tarragon does not seem to have such a good flavour.

TURKEY KIEV

0.30* £ 860 cals

* plus 45 minutes chilling

Serves 1

1 turkey breast steak, weighing at
  least 175 g (6 oz)

50 g (2 oz) butter, softened

1 very small garlic clove, skinned
  and crushed

5 ml (1 tsp) chopped fresh parsley

plain flour, for coating

½ beaten egg

30–45 ml (2–3 tbsp) oatmeal

vegetable oil, for deep frying

1 Bat out the turkey steak
between 2 sheets of dampened
greaseproof or non-stick paper,
making certain that the flesh does
not split. Check this by holding
the turkey up to the light.

2 Put the butter, garlic and
parsley in a small bowl and
cream together. Cover the bowl
and chill the butter in the
refrigerator for at least 15 minutes.

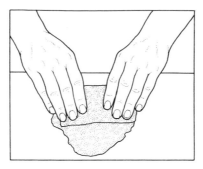

3 Place the herb butter in the
centre of the steak. Fold and
roll the flesh around the butter to
encase it completely. Secure with a
cocktail stick.

4 Roll the turkey in the flour and
shake off any excess, then dip
in the beaten egg, making sure that
the turkey is coated all over.
Finally, coat the turkey parcel
with the oatmeal. Chill in the
refrigerator again for 30 minutes.

5 Heat the oil in a deep-fat frier
to 170°C (325°F). Remove the
cocktail stick from the turkey, then
deep fry the turkey for 15–20
minutes until golden brown and
crisp. Serve as soon as possible.

6 To serve two: double the
quantity of ingredients, but
use 1 medium garlic clove. Follow
the recipe above.

Menu Suggestion
Serve with a mixed side salad or a
hot vegetable dish such as
Chakchouka (page 100).

LEMON AND MUSTARD MACKEREL

| 0.45 | £ | 940 cals |

Serves 1

50 g (2 oz) butter

½ small onion, skinned and finely chopped

50 g (2 oz) fresh breadcrumbs

15 ml (1 tbsp) whole mustard seeds

finely grated rind and juice of 1 lemon

10 ml (2 tsp) French mustard

1 egg yolk

salt and freshly ground pepper

1 mackerel, weighing about 350 g (12 oz), cleaned and gutted

about 15 ml (1 tbsp) plain flour

fresh coriander, to garnish

1 Melt 25 g (1 oz) of the butter in a small frying pan, add the onion and fry gently for about 5 minutes until soft but not coloured.

2 Turn the onion into a bowl and add the breadcrumbs, mustard seeds, lemon rind, mustard, egg yolk and salt and pepper to taste.

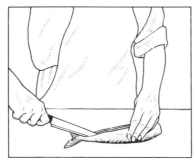

3 Cut the head off the mackerel and split open along the underside. If the inside is very black, rub with salt to remove and rinse well under cold running water.

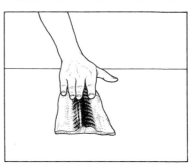

4 With the cut side down, press firmly along the back of the fish to loosen the backbone.

5 Open out the fish and cut the bone at the base of the tail. Gently pull the bone away from the flesh.

6 With a little of the remaining butter, grease a shallow ovenproof dish just large enough to hold the mackerel.

7 Press the breadcrumb mixture well into the cavity of the fish and place in the dish. Make deep slashes along the fish.

8 Dust the mackerel lightly with flour and pour over the lemon juice. Dot with the remaining butter. Cook, uncovered, in the oven at 190°C (375°F) mark 5 for about 30 minutes. Baste frequently during cooking time. Serve hot, garnished with coriander.

9 To serve two: double the quantity of ingredients but use 75 g (3 oz) butter. Follow the recipe above.

Menu Suggestion
Serve with boiled or steamed new potatoes in their skins, and a seasonal vegetable.

WHITING IN SOURED CREAM WITH TOMATOES

| 0.15 | £ | 452 cals |

Serves 1

175 g (6 oz) whiting fillet

salt and freshly ground pepper

knob of butter

1 medium, firm tomato

15 ml (1 tbsp) chopped fresh
    parsley and chives, mixed

75 ml (5 tbsp) soured cream

50 g (2 oz) Gruyère cheese, grated

sprigs of herbs, to garnish (optional)

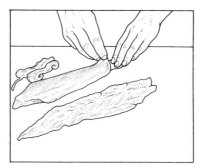

1 Skin the whiting. Dip your fingers in salt to get a good grip. Loosen a corner and pull firmly so the skin comes off cleanly.

2 Choose a shallow serving dish that fits under the grill and is just large enough to take the fish in a single layer. Put a knob of butter in the dish and grill until melted.

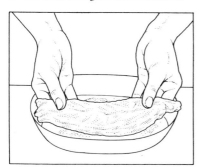

3 Remove the dish from the grill and put in the fish. Turn the fish so it is buttered side up, then sprinkle with salt and pepper to taste. Grill for 2–3 minutes.

4 Meanwhile, chop the tomato finely, place in a bowl and combine with the herbs and soured cream. Add 40 g (1½ oz) of the Gruyère cheese and salt and pepper to taste and mix again.

5 When the fish has cooked for about 3 minutes, spoon the cream mixture on top. Grate over a little more cheese and grill for a further 2 minutes, until bubbling. The sauce will not be completely smooth. Serve at once, garnished with sprigs of herbs, if liked.

6 To serve two: double the quantity of ingredients and follow the recipe above.

Menu Suggestion
Serve with a green vegetable such as French or runner beans or petits pois. Sauté potatoes or Swiss Fried Potatoes (page 104) would also go well with the fish.

WHITING IN SOURED CREAM WITH TOMATOES
Whiting is a member of the cod family, and is fished in North Atlantic waters. It is a small, round white fish which has a distinctive flavour and beautiful soft texture, but it is often overlooked for the more common cod and haddock. Like all white fish, whiting is high in protein, it also has a very low fat content and is therefore well worth looking out for, especially if you are health-conscious, or on a slimming diet.

SPICY PRAWN RISOTTO

| 0.25 | 🍱 | £ £ | 768 cals |

Serves 1

30 ml (2 tbsp) olive oil

15 g ($\frac{1}{2}$ oz) butter

1 small onion, skinned and finely chopped

1 garlic clove, skinned and crushed

1 small red chilli, seeded and finely chopped, or $\frac{1}{2}$ dried red chilli, crushed

75 g (3 oz) Italian risotto rice

350 ml (12 fl oz) hot chicken stock

2.5 ml ($\frac{1}{2}$ tsp) powdered saffron or turmeric

salt and freshly ground pepper

75 g (3 oz) peeled prawns

30 ml (2 tbsp) chopped fresh coriander or mint

whole prawns, to garnish (optional)

1 Heat the oil with the butter in a heavy-based saucepan. Add the onion, garlic and chilli and fry gently for about 5 minutes until soft but not coloured.

2 Add the rice and stir gently until coated in the onion mixture. Add about one-third of the hot stock, the saffron or turmeric and salt and pepper to taste. Stir over gentle heat until the liquid has been absorbed.

3 Continue adding more stock and stirring until all the liquid has been absorbed and the rice is *al dente* (tender, but firm to the bite). The total cooking time should be about 20 minutes.

4 Add the prawns and coriander and fold gently to mix with the rice. Heat through, then taste and adjust seasoning. Serve hot, adding a garnish of whole prawns, if liked.

5 To serve two: follow the recipe above, doubling the quantity of rice, stock, prawns and coriander.

Menu Suggestion

Spicy Prawn Risotto tastes good with a refreshing side salad of thinly sliced cucumber dressed in olive oil, wine vinegar and chopped fresh coriander or mint.

PIZZA MARINARA

| 0.45 | 🍴 ✳* | 1054 cals |

* freeze at the end of step 4, before
baking

Serves 1

½ quantity of Quick Pizza Dough
(page 158)

225 g (8 oz) can tomatoes

10 ml (2 tsp) tomato purée

10 ml (2 tsp) chopped fresh basil or
5 ml (½ tsp) dried

salt and freshly ground pepper

99 g (3½ oz) can tuna fish, drained

50 g (2 oz) Mozzarella, Gruyère or
Cheddar cheese

4 canned anchovy fillets, drained

2 black olives, stoned and halved

15 ml (1 tbsp) olive oil

basil sprigs, to garnish

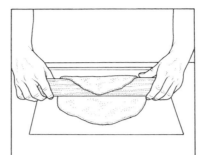

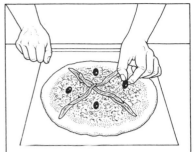

1 Roll out the dough to a 27.5 cm (11 inch) round. Place the round on a greased baking sheet and set aside.

2 Put the tomatoes and juice in a blender with the tomato purée, half of the basil and salt and pepper to taste. Work until smooth, then spread over the pizza base, right to the edges.

3 Flake the tuna with a fork, then scatter evenly over the pizza. Slice the Mozzarella or grate the Gruyère or Cheddar. Cover the tuna with the cheese.

4 Arrange the anchovies on top of the pizza in the shape of a cross, then place 1 olive half in each quarter.

5 Mix the oil with the remaining basil and drizzle over the pizza. Bake in the oven at 220°C (425°F) mark 7 for 25 minutes. Serve hot, garnished with basil sprigs.

6 To serve two: use the full quantity of Quick Pizza Dough (page 158), to make two 27.5 cm (11 inch) pizzas. Follow the recipe above for the topping, using a 200 g (7 oz) can tuna, 100 g (4 oz) cheese, 8 anchovy fillets, 4 olives and 30 ml (2 tbsp) olive oil. Make the tomato sauce spread over the 2 pizzas by diluting it with wine, stock or water.

Menu Suggestion

Serve with a crisp mixed salad of fennel, radicchio and lettuce tossed in a dressing of olive oil, lemon juice and crushed garlic.

PIZZA MARINARA

Italian Mozzarella was originally a buffalo milk cheese, but these days it is most likely to be made from cow's milk. It is a fresh cheese, usually sold in a waxed paper wrapping in Italian delicatessens. Mozzarella has a unique melting quality, and is the traditional cheese for pizza toppings. If you find it difficult to buy genuine Italian Mozzarella, however, look for the Danish and Scottish equivalents. These are sold in most supermarkets and although they are much firmer in texture, they make good substitutes. Gruyère or Cheddar can also be used instead of Mozzarella, so too can the Italian Bel Paese, which melts well and has a mild, fruity flavour.

FETTUCCINE IN CREAMY HAM AND MUSHROOM SAUCE

| 0.20 | £ | 1134 cals |

Serves 1

100–175 g (4–6 oz) fresh or dried
   fettuccine or tagliatelle
salt and freshly ground pepper
25 g (1 oz) butter or margarine
40 g (1½ oz) button mushrooms,
   finely sliced
1 slice smoked ham, cut into fine
   strips
freshly grated nutmeg
75 ml (5 tbsp) double cream
25 g (1 oz) freshly grated Parmesan
   cheese

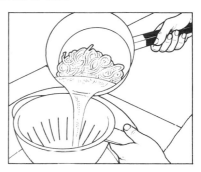

1 Put the pasta in a large pan of
   boiling salted water and cook
for 8–12 minutes if using dried
pasta, 2–3 minutes if using fresh.

2 Meanwhile, melt the butter in
   a small saucepan, add the
mushrooms and fry for 2–3
minutes. Add the strips of ham
and nutmeg, salt and pepper to
taste. Stir in the cream and
simmer for 2 minutes or until
slightly thickened.

3 Drain the pasta and stir in the
   sauce and Parmesan cheese,
coating the pasta evenly. Serve
immediately.

4 To serve two: double the
   quantity of ingredients and
follow the recipe above.

Menu Suggestion
Serve with extra grated Parmesan
cheese and plenty of freshly
ground black pepper. An Italian-
style salad of cold French beans,
tomato, onion, garlic and black
olives would go well with the
pasta, tossed in a dressing of olive
oil, lemon juice, chopped fresh
basil and salt and pepper.

**FETTUCCINE IN CREAMY
HAM AND MUSHROOM
SAUCE**
To give this dish an authentic
Italian flavour, use Parma ham,
which tastes both sweet and
smoky at the same time.
Although it is expensive, you
only need a very small quantity.
Genuine Parma ham comes from
the area around the town of
Parma in northern Italy, and can
be identified by the words
prosciutto di Parma which are
branded into its skin. Two other
hams which you could also use,
but which are less expensive than
Parma, are *coppa* and *prosciutto
di San Daniele*.

Special Occasions For Two

Whether it is a romantic candlelit dinner party or a special Sunday lunch, you can really go to town if you are cooking for two. Luxurious ingredients like scallops, game, duck and fillet steak are just perfect for two people, and in this chapter you will find extra special ways of cooking them.

BUTTERED SALMON STEAKS

| 0.35 | £ £ | 640 cals |

Serves 2

100 g (4 oz) butter, softened

finely grated rind and juice of
  $\frac{1}{2}$ lemon

10 ml (2 tsp) chopped fresh
  tarragon or 5 ml (1 tsp) dried

2 fresh salmon steaks, each
  weighing about 175 g (6 oz)

75 ml (5 tbsp) dry white wine

freshly ground pepper

tarragon sprigs and lemon
  wedges, to serve

1 In a small bowl, cream together
the butter, lemon rind and
juice and the tarragon.

2 Cut 2 pieces of foil, each one
large enough to wrap around a
salmon steak. Grease the foil with
half of the butter mixture.

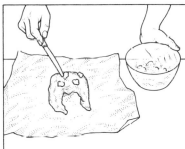

3 Place the salmon steaks on the
buttered foil and dot with the
remaining butter. Spoon the wine
over the steaks and sprinkle with
pepper to taste.

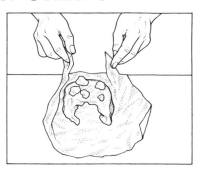

4 Fold the foil around the steaks,
keeping the parcels quite loose.
Place the parcels on a baking sheet
and bake in the oven at 170°C
(325°F) mark 3 for 20 minutes, or
until the fish is firm.

5 Unwrap the salmon steaks,
place on warmed individual
serving plates and pour over the
juices from the foil packets. Serve
immediately, garnished with
tarragon sprigs and lemon wedges.

Menu Suggestion
Serve with buttered new potatoes
and a special green vegetable such
as mangetout, petits pois or
broccoli. The ideal wine to serve
would be a crisp, dry white such as
a French Muscadet or Italian
Verdicchio.

BUTTERED SALMON STEAKS

Called the 'king of the river', the
salmon is a much-prized fish —
and one of the most expensive.
The salmon is a marine fish, but
it is hatched in fresh water,
where it spends the first three or
four years of its life. After this
the salmon migrates to the sea
and does not return to its native
river until a few years later where
it usually dies after spawning. If
you see fish sold by the name of
grilse, this is a salmon that has
only spent one year at sea.
Salmon trout are similar, in that
they do not spend as much time
at sea as the true salmon. Both
grilse and salmon trout are less
expensive than the true salmon,
and are well worth asking for at
your fishmonger.

POACHED TROUT WITH FENNEL

| 1.00 | £ £ | 465 cals |

Serves 2

1 small head Florence fennel,
weighing about 175 g (6 oz)

350 g (12 oz) potatoes, peeled and
thinly sliced

1 bay leaf

60 ml (4 tbsp) dry vermouth

salt and freshly ground pepper

25 g (1 oz) butter or margarine

2 fresh trout, each weighing about
225 g (8 oz), cleaned

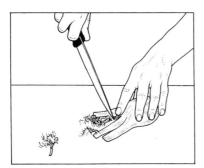

1 Trim the green feathery leaves
from the fennel and reserve for
the garnish. Slice the fennel thinly
and scatter over the bottom of a
shallow ovenproof dish.

2 Cover the fennel with the
slices of potato and place the
bay leaf on top. Pour over the
vermouth and 60 ml (4 tbsp)
water, then sprinkle with salt and
pepper to taste.

3 Place the prepared trout on top
of the fennel and potato and
dot with the butter.

4 Cover tightly with foil and
bake in the oven at 180°C
(350°F) mark 4 for about
40 minutes.

5 Remove the foil to serve. Chop
the reserved fennel tops finely,
then sprinkle over the dish. Serve
immediately.

Menu Suggestion
With fennel and potatoes
incorporated in the dish, this
trout needs only a simple
accompaniment such as a colourful
mixed salad or seasonal vegetable.
A crisp Californian Sauvignon
Blanc is a good white wine to serve
with fish such as trout.

POACHED TROUT WITH FENNEL

Florence fennel is an interesting-
looking vegetable, rather like a
squat celery topped with feathery
leaves. It is called Florence or
Florentine fennel because it
originated around the city of
Florence in northern Italy, and
this also distinguishes it from the
herb of the same name. When
buying Florence fennel, look for
white or pale green heads. The
dark, green fennel can taste
rather bitter. Florence fennel has
a flavour like aniseed or mild
liquorice, which goes particularly
well with the delicate flavour of
fish, especially trout. To
accentuate the aniseed flavour of
this dish, try substituting the
vermouth with Pernod or Pastis,
two aniseed-flavoured drinks
from France.

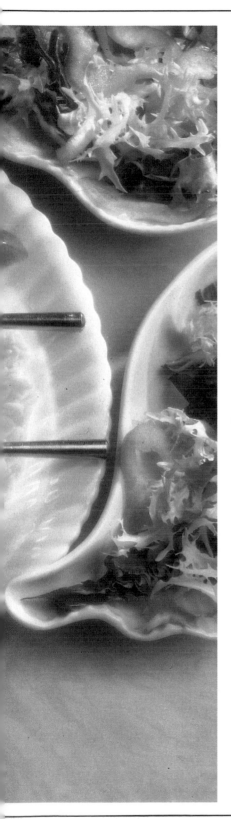

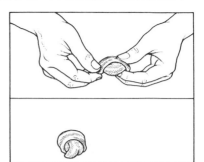

SKEWERED SCALLOPS WITH BACON

| *0.25* | £ £ | 443 cals |

Serves 2

8 large fresh or frozen scallops, thawed

4 rashers of streaky bacon, rinded

15 ml (1 tbsp) chopped fresh basil or tarragon or 5 ml (1 tsp) dried

30 ml (2 tbsp) olive or vegetable oil

2 medium tomatoes, skinned

5 ml (1 tsp) wine vinegar

salt and freshly ground pepper

basil sprigs, to garnish

1 If necessary, remove and discard the tough white 'muscle' from each scallop, which is found opposite the orange coral. Separate the corals.

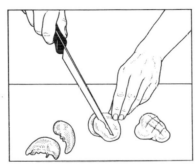

2 With a sharp knife, lightly score the scallops on each side in a lattice pattern.

3 Stretch the bacon rashers with the back of a knife and divide each rasher in two.

4 Wrap the bacon around the corals. Thread the scallops horizontally and corals alternately on to 2 kebab skewers. Place in a foil-lined grill pan.

5 Mix the basil with 15 ml (1 tbsp) of the oil and brush over the scallops and bacon. Cook under a hot grill for 5 minutes on each side until the scallops are just cooked and the bacon golden, brushing with more oil and basil when turning the skewers over.

6 Slice each tomato into 6 wedges and arrange on the side of 2 individual serving plates. Whisk the remaining oil and the vinegar together, with salt and pepper to taste.

7 When the scallops are cooked, place a skewer on each plate and spoon the dressing over the tomatoes. Garnish with sprigs of basil and serve immediately.

Menu Suggestion

Serve on a bed of saffron rice, with side salads of curly endive, radicchio and chopped red or green peppers. A chilled dry white Bordeaux wine such as Entre-Deux-Mers goes well with scallops.

FILETS DE BOEUF EN CROÛTE
(BEEF FILLETS IN PASTRY)

0.45*	£ £	871 cals

*plus 30 minutes chilling

Serves 2

2 fillet steaks, each about 2.5 cm
 (1 inch) thick

15 ml (1 tbsp) vegetable oil

200 g (7½ oz) packet frozen puff
 pastry, thawed

225 g (8 oz) fresh gooseberries

about 30 ml (2 tbsp) granulated
 sugar, to taste

1 egg, size 4, beaten

watercress sprigs, to garnish

1 Trim the fillet steaks of any
 excess fat. Heat the oil in a
small frying pan, add the steaks
and brown for a few seconds to
seal. Remove and cool.

2 Roll out the pastry on a floured
 work surface until 0.25 cm
(⅛ inch) thick. Cut in half.

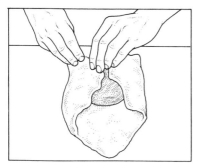

3 Place 1 steak on each piece of
 pastry. Fold the pastry over
the steaks, moistening and sealing
the edges well.

4 Trim off any excess pastry and
 use the trimmings to decorate
the parcels.

5 Place the parcels on a baking
 sheet, cover and chill in the
refrigerator for about 30 minutes.

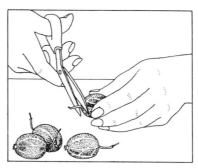

6 Meanwhile, prepare the sauce.
 Top and tail the gooseberries,
then rinse under cold running
water and place in a small
saucepan with 30 ml (2 tbsp) sugar
and 60 ml (4 tbsp) water. Cover
tightly and simmer until soft.

7 Press the contents of the pan
 through a nylon sieve to
remove all pips, then return the
purée to a clean saucepan. Add a
little more sugar if necessary, but
the sauce should be tart.

8 Uncover the steaks and glaze
 with beaten egg. Bake in the
oven at 220°C (425°F) mark 7 for
about 15 minutes for medium
rare, 20 minutes for medium to
well done (depending on the
thickness of the steaks). Reheat the
sauce to serve.

Menu Suggestion
Serve for a very special celebration
meal with French fries or sauté
potatoes if you like them, and a
seasonal green vegetable or salad.
A good-quality red Burgundy or
Côtes du Rhône would be the ideal
wine to serve.

LAMB NOISETTES IN PORT AND REDCURRANT SAUCE

| 1.15 | £ £ | ✳ | 527 cals |

Serves 2

4 lamb noisettes

plain flour, for coating

25 g (1 oz) butter

15 ml (1 tbsp) vegetable oil

1 small onion, skinned and finely chopped

1 garlic clove, skinned and crushed

60 ml (4 tbsp) ruby port

300 ml ($\frac{1}{2}$ pint) chicken stock

1 bay leaf

salt and freshly ground pepper

30 ml (2 tbsp) redcurrant jelly

fresh bay leaves, to garnish (optional)

1 Lightly coat the lamb noisettes with flour. Heat the butter and oil in a small flameproof casserole. Add the noisettes and brown quickly on both sides. Remove from the casserole with a slotted spoon and set aside.

2 Add the onion and garlic to the casserole and fry for about 5 minutes until golden. Stir in the port, stock and bay leaf. Season well with salt and pepper.

3 Replace the noisettes and bring to the boil, then cover and simmer gently for about 40 minutes until tender, turning the meat once during this time.

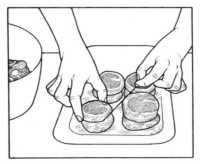

4 Lift the noisettes out of the sauce and remove the string. Place the noisettes on a warmed serving dish and keep hot.

5 Add the redcurrant jelly to the liquid in the casserole and boil rapidly for 5–10 minutes to reduce the sauce to about 150 ml ($\frac{1}{4}$ pint). Taste and adjust seasoning, remove the bay leaf, then pour the sauce over the noisettes. Serve immediately, garnished with fresh bay leaves, if liked.

Menu Suggestion
Serve with a special French potato dish such as a *gratin dauphinois* and a green vegetable like courgettes or mangetout tossed in butter and chopped fresh herbs.

SPICED INDONESIAN PORK

| 0.35* | ✳* | 320 cals |

*plus at least 2 hours or overnight marinating; freeze in the marinade

Serves 2

1 large pork fillet (tenderloin), weighing about 350 g (12 oz)

30 ml (2 tbsp) dark soy sauce

15 ml (1 tbsp) honey

5 ml (1 tsp) five spice powder

½ small onion, skinned and grated

1 garlic clove, skinned and crushed

juice of ½ lemon

lemon wedges, to serve

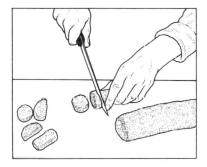

1 Cut the pork into cubes, then cut these in half to make thin chunks. Place in a bowl with the remaining ingredients except the lemon wedges, then stir well to mix. Cover and leave to marinate for at least 2 hours, or overnight.

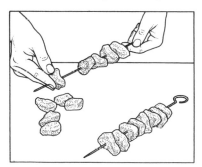

2 When ready to cook, preheat the grill to moderate. Thread the pieces of pork on to 2 or 4 oiled kebab skewers.

3 Put the skewers in the grill pan and grill for 15–20 minutes, turning frequently and brushing with any remaining marinade. Serve hot, with lemon wedges.

Menu Suggestion

Spiced Indonesian Pork both looks and tastes good on a bed of spiced aromatic rice. If you like, you can also serve it with a simple peanut sauce: heat together 60 ml (4 tbsp) crunchy peanut butter, 30 ml (2 tbsp) desiccated coconut, 10 ml (2 tsp) dark soft brown sugar, 1.25 ml (¼ tsp) chilli powder and enough water to give a thick or pouring consistency.

SPICED INDONESIAN PORK

For a summer barbecue meal, these kebabs look more authentically Indonesian if cooked on bamboo skewers, which can be bought at Chinese and other oriental specialist shops. Soak the bamboo skewers in warm water for about 30 minutes before using (this is to prevent them scorching during cooking), then thread only a few pieces of meat on the top two-thirds of each skewer. Barbecue over hot charcoal for 10 minutes.

ESCALOPES DE VEAU FLAMBÉ
(FLAMED VEAL ESCALOPES)

| 0.20 | 🍳 | £ £ | 500 cals |

Serves 2

2 veal escalopes

25 g (1 oz) butter

15 ml (1 tbsp) olive oil

30 ml (2 tbsp) Calvados or brandy

2 crisp dessert apples

60 ml (4 tbsp) dry white wine

30 ml (2 tbsp) double cream

salt and freshly ground pepper

1 Cut each escalope in half and place between 2 sheets of dampened greaseproof paper. Beat out thinly with a rolling pin.

2 Melt the butter with the oil in a large, heavy-based frying pan. Add the escalopes and fry over moderate heat for 5–7 minutes until the meat is tender, turning once.

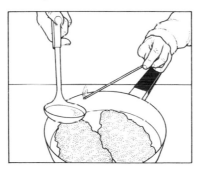

3 Warm the Calvados or brandy gently in a ladle or small saucepan. Remove the pan of escalopes from the heat. Ignite the Calvados or brandy and pour over the escalopes while still flaming.

4 When the flames have died down, remove the escalopes from the pan with a fish slice. Place on a warmed serving plate, cover and keep hot in a low oven.

5 Quarter and core the apples, then slice thickly. Add the white wine to the pan and stir to scrape up the sediment with the pan juices. Add the apple slices and toss over high heat for about 5 minutes until tender and lightly coloured.

6 With a slotted spoon, remove the apple slices from the pan juices and arrange with the veal. Stir the cream into the pan juices and heat through. Add salt and pepper to taste, then pour over the veal and apples. Serve promptly.

Menu Suggestion
Simple, but very rich, this main course dish is best served with plain accompaniments. Lightly steamed mangetout, broccoli or French beans would go very well, or a dressed simple green salad.

ESCALOPES DE VEAU FLAMBÉ
Calvados is an apple brandy from Normandy in north-western France. It is one of the most highly prized of French brandies, with its own *appellation contrôleé*. Only apple brandies made in the *appellation* region are entitled to call themselves by the name of Calvados—others must be content with the name *eau-de-vie de cidre*. The Normans drink a great deal of Calvados as a digestif after meals, they also use it extensively in cooking.

POUSSINS WITH CREAM AND GRAPES

| 1.15 | ▯ | £ £ | 552 cals |

Serves 2

2 oven-ready poussins

50 g (2 oz) butter

2 sprigs of fresh tarragon or 5 ml (1 tsp) dried

salt and freshly ground pepper

100 g (4 oz) muscat or other green grapes

60 ml (4 tbsp) dry white wine or sherry

60 ml (4 tbsp) double cream

tarragon or watercress sprigs, to garnish

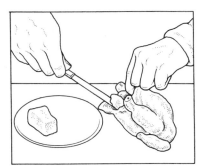

1 Wash the poussins inside and out, then pat dry with absorbent kitchen paper. Put a knob of butter inside each bird, then the tarragon and salt and pepper to taste.

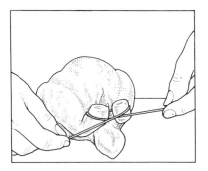

2 Truss each bird with fine string or trussing thread, then spread the remaining butter over the breast of each bird.

3 Place the poussins side by side in a roasting tin and roast in the oven at 180°C (350°F) mark 4 for 1 hour, or until the juice runs clear and the flesh feels tender when the thickest part of the thighs is pierced with a skewer.

4 Meanwhile, put the grapes in a bowl, pour in boiling water and leave to stand for 20 seconds. Drain and plunge into cold water. Peel off the skins, then halve the grapes and remove the pips.

5 Transfer the poussins to a warmed serving plate and remove the trussing string or thread. Cover loosely and keep hot in a very low oven.

6 Transfer the roasting tin to the top of the cooker and pour in the wine or sherry. Stir to scrape up the sediment from the base of the tin, then add the cream and prepared grapes. Heat through gently, stirring all the time, then taste and adjust seasoning.

7 Pour a little of the sauce over the poussins and garnish with the tarragon or watercress sprigs. Serve immediately, with the remaining sauce in a sauce boat.

Menu Suggestion
Serve this rich main course with plain accompaniments such as boiled new potatoes in their skins and a crisp green salad.

PEKING DUCK WITH PANCAKES

2.00* □ □ £ £ 1094 cals

* plus overnight hanging

Serves 2

2 kg (4 lb) oven-ready duckling, cleaned

60 ml (4 tbsp) dark soft brown sugar

30 ml (2 tbsp) soy sauce

100 g (4 oz) plain flour

salt

a little vegetable oil, for brushing

hoisin sauce, cucumber and spring onions, to serve

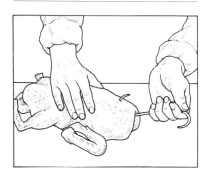

1 Wash the duckling well inside and out, then pat thoroughly dry with absorbent kitchen paper. Insert a meat hook in the neck.

2 Put the sugar and soy sauce in a saucepan with 300 ml ($\frac{1}{2}$ pint) water. Heat gently until the sugar has dissolved, then boil for 5 minutes. Remove from the heat.

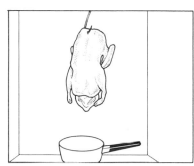

3 Brush the sugar syrup over the skin of the duckling several times. Hang the bird up in a cool, airy place with a pan underneath to catch any drips. Leave overnight.

4 The next day, put the duckling on a rack in a roasting tin and pour water underneath to cover the bottom of the tin. Roast the duckling in the oven at 200°C (400°F) mark 6 for $1\frac{1}{2}$ hours.

5 Meanwhile, make the pancakes. Mix the flour and a pinch of salt in a bowl, then pour in 120 ml (4 fl oz) boiling water. Stir vigorously to a stiff dough with chopsticks or a wooden spoon.

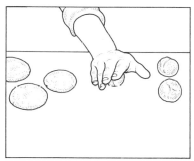

6 Divide the dough into 6 equal pieces. Roll each piece into a ball, then flatten with the heel of your hand and roll out to a 6 cm ($2\frac{1}{2}$ inch) round.

7 Brush 3 of the rounds with a little oil, then sandwich the remaining rounds on top. Roll out each 'sandwich' on a lightly floured surface until 15 cm (6 inches) in diameter. Cover with a damp, clean tea-towel.

8 When the duckling is cooked, transfer to a warmed serving platter and keep hot in the oven turned to its lowest setting.

9 Heat a small, heavy-based frying pan until very hot. Add 1 pancake 'sandwich' and cook until air bubbles appear on the surface. Turn over and repeat cooking on the other side.

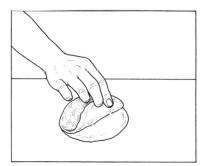

10 Remove the pancakes from the pan and carefully peel them apart. Fold in half, place on a plate and cover with a damp, clean tea-towel. Repeat until all the pancakes are cooked.

11 Serve the duckling and pancakes hot, with hoisin sauce, spring onions and cucumber handed separately.

PEKING DUCK WITH PANCAKES

Peking duck is the perfect main course for an informal Chinese-style supper party. Each person helps themselves to a pancake, spreads a little hoisin sauce over, then tops it with a few slices of duck meat and crispy skin and a few pieces of spring onion and cucumber. The pancake is then rolled up neatly around the filling and eaten with the fingers.

Hoisin sauce, sometimes also called barbecue sauce, is available in bottles from oriental specialist shops and some large supermarkets; once opened, store it in the refrigerator.

TRADITIONAL ROAST PARTRIDGE

| 1.20 | 🍳 £ £ | 366 cals |

Serves 2

2 juniper berries

2 allspice berries

1 clove

75 g (3 oz) crustless bread

finely grated rind and juice of
   1 large orange

finely grated rind and juice of
   1 large lemon

2.5 ml ($\frac{1}{2}$ tsp) dried marjoram

2.5 ml ($\frac{1}{2}$ tsp) dried thyme

10 ml (2 tsp) chopped fresh parsley

salt and freshly ground pepper

1 egg, size 5 or 6, beaten

1–2 young partridges, depending
   on size

2 rashers of streaky bacon

30 ml (2 tbsp) brandy

300 ml ($\frac{1}{2}$ pint) chicken stock

watercress and game chips, to
   serve

1 First make the stuffing. Crush the juniper, allspice and clove with a pestle and mortar. Place in a bowl. Crumble in the bread with your fingers, then add the orange and lemon rinds, half of the orange juice, all of the lemon juice, the herbs and salt and pepper to taste. Mix well with your hands, then bind with the beaten egg.

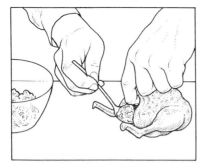

2 Wash the partridge inside and out, then pat dry with absorbent kitchen paper. Fill the body cavity of the bird with the stuffing, then truss with fine string or thread. Place the bacon rashers over the breast and secure with trussing string or thread.

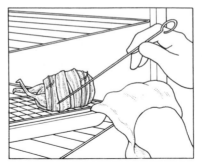

3 Place the bird in a roasting tin and roast in the oven at 190°C (375°F) mark 5 for 1 hour, or until the flesh feels tender when the thickest part of the thigh is pierced with a fine skewer. Take out of the oven and remove the trussing string or thread and the bacon. Return to the oven for a further 5 minutes to brown the breast.

4 Warm the brandy gently in a ladle or small pan, then remove from the heat and ignite. Pour over the partridge while flaming.

5 When the flames have died down, transfer the partridge to a warmed serving plate. Cover loosely and keep hot in the oven turned to its lowest setting.

6 Transfer the roasting tin to the top of the cooker and pour in the stock and remaining orange juice. Stir well to scrape up any sediment from the base and sides of the tin, then bring to the boil. Add salt and pepper to taste, then pour into a gravy boat.

7 Garnish the partridge with the watercress and game chips before serving. Hand the gravy separately.

Menu Suggestion
Serve this traditional dish with seasonal vegetables such as Brussels sprouts and carrots. Roast potatoes can also be served, if wished.

CALF'S LIVER WITH SAGE AND AVOCADO

| 0.15 | £ £ | 604 cals |

Serves 2

2 thin slices of calf's liver, each weighing 75–100 g (3–4 oz)

15 ml (1 tbsp) plain flour

10 ml (2 tsp) rubbed fresh sage or 5 ml (1 tsp) dried

salt and freshly ground pepper

50 g (2 oz) butter

1 ripe avocado

juice of 1 lime

60 ml (4 tbsp) dry vermouth

lime slices, to garnish

1 Cut the liver into small serving pieces, then coat in the flour mixed with half of the sage and pepper to taste. (Do not add salt as this will toughen the liver.)

2 Melt the butter in a heavy-based frying pan, add the liver and fry over moderate heat for 2–3 minutes on each side. Remove the pan from the heat and lift out the liver with a fish slice. Place on a warmed serving plate, cover and keep hot in a low oven.

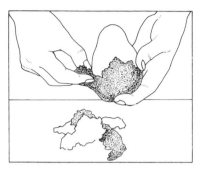

3 Peel, halve and stone the avocado. Cut the flesh into thin slices. Reheat the butter in the frying pan, add the avocado slices and fry for 1–2 minutes until heated through. Remove from the pan with a slotted spoon and arrange with the liver.

4 Pour the lime juice and vermouth into the pan, increase the heat and boil to reduce, stirring vigorously to scrape up any sediment. Add the remaining sage, taste and adjust seasoning, then pour over the liver. Serve immediately, garnished with the lime slices.

Menu Suggestion
Serve with new potatoes boiled in their skins, and a colourful vegetable such as carrots tossed in a little cream.

CALF'S LIVER WITH SAGE AND AVOCADO

Calf's liver is considered a great delicacy by gourmets, and this is reflected in its price! A little goes a long way, however, as it is a very rich meat, and in nutritional terms there is nothing to compare with it. Liver, and calf's liver especially, is exceptionally lean and tender, high in protein, low in fat, rich in iron, vitamins A and B and minerals.

Nutritionists advise that liver should be included in a healthy diet at least once a week.

Take great care when cooking calf's liver. It has a very delicate texture and should be cooked for the minimum amount of time as in this recipe, so that the centre is still moist and slightly pink. Never overcook calf's liver or it will be tough and rubbery.

Vegetables and Salads

Fresh vegetables and salads are an absolute must for a healthy diet, but it is all too easy to overlook them when you are only cooking for one or two people. The recipes in this chapter are too tempting to resist, and many of them will make complete meals in themselves.

POTATO, CARROT AND ONION CASSEROLE

| 1.15 | £ | 477 cals |

Serves 2

25 g (1 oz) butter or margarine

15 ml (1 tbsp) vegetable oil

15 ml (1 tbsp) demerara sugar

225 g (8 oz) carrots, peeled and thickly sliced

225 g (8 oz) small onions, skinned

450 g (1 lb) small new potatoes, scrubbed and cut in half

125 g (4 oz) button mushrooms

15 ml (1 tbsp) plain flour

150 ml ($\frac{1}{4}$ pint) red wine

10 ml (2 tsp) tomato purée

150 ml ($\frac{1}{4}$ pint) vegetable stock

1 bay leaf

salt and freshly ground pepper

chopped fresh parsley, to garnish

1 Heat the butter and oil together in a flameproof casserole. Add the sugar, carrots, onions and potatoes. Cook, stirring, over high heat for 5 minutes until the vegetables colour.

2 Add the mushrooms and cook for a further minute. Stir in the flour, scraping any sediment from the bottom of the pan, then add the red wine, tomato purée, stock, bay leaf and salt and pepper to taste.

3 Cover the casserole tightly, then bake in the oven at 190°C (375°F) mark 5 for about 1 hour or until the vegetables are tender.

4 Remove the bay leaf. Taste and adjust the seasoning and sprinkle with chopped parsley. Serve immediately.

Menu Suggestion
This vegetable casserole is the perfect dish to cook in the oven while you are roasting meat or cooking a meat or poultry casserole for a main course.

SOUFFLÉED CAULIFLOWER

| 0.40 | £ | 1044 cals |

Serves 1

175 g (6 oz) cauliflower florets
salt and freshly ground pepper
25 g (1 oz) butter
75 ml (5 tbsp) thick mayonnaise
5 ml (1 tsp) Dijon mustard
finely grated rind of ½ lemon
2 eggs, separated
50 g (2 oz) Cheddar cheese, grated
sprig of parsley, to garnish

1 Cook the cauliflower florets in boiling salted water for about 5 minutes—they should retain their crispness. Drain well.

2 Butter a small, shallow ovenproof dish and place the cauliflower in the bottom.

3 Put the mayonnaise, mustard and lemon rind in a medium bowl, stir in the egg yolks and 25 g (1 oz) of the grated cheese. Season with salt and pepper to taste.

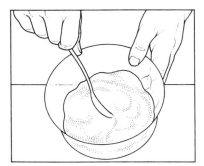

4 Put the egg whites in a separate bowl and whisk until stiff. Fold the egg whites carefully into the mayonnaise mixture.

5 Spoon this mixture over the cauliflower, sprinkle with the remaining cheese and bake in the oven at 190°C (375°F) mark 5 for about 25 minutes or until risen and golden. Serve immediately, garnished with a sprig of parsley.

6 To serve two: double the quantity of ingredients, but use 3 eggs and 75 g (3 oz) Cheddar cheese. Follow the recipe above.

Menu Suggestion
This delicious cauliflower dish can be served as an accompaniment to a grilled chop, chicken portion or steak. It would also make a good light lunch or supper dish, with wholemeal French-style bread.

SOUFFLÉED CAULIFLOWER

The French Dijon mustard specified in this recipe is a smooth, mild-flavoured mustard which will not override the other, delicate flavours of this dish. Made in the town of Dijon in the region of Burgundy, *moutarde à la Dijonnaise* is unique in that it is made from mustard grains mixed with verjuice (the juice of sour Burgundy grapes), plus herbs and flavourings. Most other mustards are made with vinegar, which is why they are sharper in flavour than Dijon.

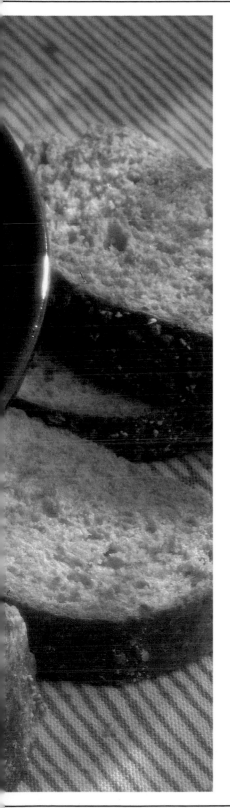

LENTIL HOT POT

0.25	£	637 cals

Serves 2

175 g (6 oz) green lentils

salt and freshly ground pepper

25 g (1 oz) butter or margarine

1 medium onion, skinned and chopped

2.5 ml ($\frac{1}{2}$ tsp) curry powder

125 g (4 oz) celery, trimmed and sliced

125 g (4 oz) carrots, peeled and sliced

15 ml (1 tbsp) plain flour

1 chicken stock cube

125 g (4 oz) French beans, topped and tailed

125 g (4 oz) courgettes, sliced

25 g (1 oz) fresh breadcrumbs

75 g (3 oz) Cheddar cheese, grated

1 Cook the lentils in boiling salted water for 20 minutes or until tender. Drain well.

2 Meanwhile, melt the butter in a large saucepan, add the onion and fry for about 5 minutes until soft but not coloured. Add the curry powder, celery and carrots, cover and cook gently for 5 minutes.

3 Stir in the flour, stock cube and 300 ml ($\frac{1}{2}$ pint) water. Bring to the boil, stirring. Season with salt and pepper to taste and simmer for 5 minutes.

4 Add the French beans and simmer for a further 5 minutes, then add the courgettes. Continue cooking for about 10 minutes or until the vegetables are tender, but still have bite.

5 Drain the lentils and add to the vegetables. Heat through for 2–3 minutes. Taste and adjust seasoning, then turn into a deep ovenproof dish.

6 Mix the breadcrumbs and cheese together and sprinkle on top. Put under a preheated hot grill until crisp and golden brown. Serve hot.

Menu Suggestion

Lentil Hot Pot goes especially well with smoked or spicy sausages. It can also be served as a vegetarian dish, in which case serve wholemeal bread to make a more nutritious meal. Substitute vegetable stock for the chicken stock.

LENTIL HOT POT

Lentils come in so many different shapes and sizes that it is very easy to become confused about the correct ones to use for a particular recipe. This warming winter hot pot calls for green lentils, which you will find in health food shops, Indian stores and continental delicatessens. They are whole, with quite a pronounced 'earthy' flavour. The beauty of this type of lentil is that it keeps its shape during cooking, unlike the split red and yellow varieties, which quickly disintegrate to a mush. Another plus point with lentils is that they do not need to be soaked like other pulses; they are also extremely nutritious in that they are high in protein and fibre, yet low in fat.

CHAKCHOUKA
(MOROCCAN VEGETABLE STEW)

| 1.00 | ✳ | 337 cals |

Serves 2

| 1 small aubergine |
| salt and freshly ground pepper |
| 1 red pepper |
| 1 green pepper |
| 225 g (8 oz) tomatoes |
| 1 medium onion, skinned and thinly sliced |
| 1 garlic clove, skinned and crushed |
| 1 fresh green chilli or 2.5 ml (½ tsp) chilli powder |
| 60 ml (4 tbsp) olive oil |

1 Slice the aubergine thinly, then place in a colander, sprinkling each layer with salt. Cover with a plate, put heavy weights on top and leave to dégorge for 20–30 minutes while preparing the other vegetables.

2 Put the peppers under a preheated moderate grill and cook until the skins char on all sides, turning them frequently.

3 Remove the peppers from the grill and wrap immediately in absorbent kitchen paper. Cool.

4 Skin the tomatoes. Plunge them into boiling water, then into cold. Peel off the skins and chop the flesh roughly. Halve the chilli, if using, remove the seeds under cold running water, then chop the flesh finely.

5 Rinse the aubergine slices under cold running water, then pat dry with absorbent kitchen paper. Heat the oil in a heavy-based saucepan, add the sliced onion, crushed garlic and fresh chilli, if using, and fry gently for about 5 minutes until soft but not coloured.

6 Add the aubergine slices, the chopped tomato, chilli powder, if using, salt and pepper to taste. Cook for 20 minutes, stirring frequently.

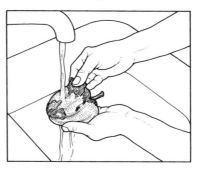

7 Meanwhile, unwrap the peppers and peel off the skins by rubbing with your fingers under cold running water. Discard the cores and seeds, then pat the flesh dry with absorbent kitchen paper. Cut into thin strips.

8 Add the pepper strips to the pan and heat through for about 5 minutes. Taste and adjust seasoning before serving.

Menu Suggestion
Serve as an unusual alternative to ratatouille, with roast or grilled steak and chops. In Morocco, Chakchouka is often served as a lunch or supper dish with eggs, which are either dropped into the vegetables and cooked whole for the last few minutes of the cooking time, or stirred in until creamy.

CHAKCHOUKA

Chakchouka is a spicy, Moroccan version of the well-known French vegetable dish, ratatouille. Like ratatouille, it keeps extremely well and seems to taste even better if stored in the refrigerator for 2–3 days before eating. In this recipe, it is served hot as a vegetable accompaniment, but it tastes just as good served chilled as a starter, with crusty French bread and butter and a bottle of chilled dry white wine.

Although it is time-consuming to have to dégorge the aubergine, try not to skimp on this part of the preparation. Salting the aubergine flesh draws out the bitter juices from the vegetable; if these are not extracted the finished dish may be spoilt.

Grilling peppers until charred, then wrapping them in kitchen paper until cold, and then peeling them, gives them a wonderful smoky flavour and soft, juicy texture. It is a favourite way of preparing peppers on the continent and in the Middle East and Africa. In summertime they can be charred on the barbecue, in which case they will taste even better.

COURGETTES AND ALMONDS

| 0.10 | £ | 365 cals |

Serves 1

2 medium courgettes

25 g (1 oz) butter

finely grated rind and juice of ½ lemon

salt and freshly ground pepper

25 g (1 oz) flaked almonds

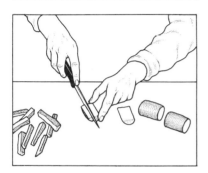

1 Slice the courgettes in 3 horizontally. Halve the slices and cut into fingers.

2 Melt the butter in a frying pan, add the courgettes, lemon rind and juice, and salt and pepper to taste. Cook over moderate heat, stirring from time to time, for about 5 minutes or until the courgette fingers turn opaque. Remove from the heat.

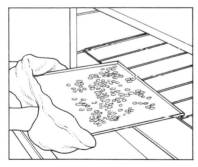

3 Spread the flaked almonds on a baking sheet and toast under a preheated hot grill until golden. Add the almonds to the courgettes, return to the heat and cook, stirring, for a further minute until heated through. Serve immediately.

4 To serve two: double the quantity of ingredients and follow the recipe above.

Menu Suggestion

Courgettes and Almonds goes especially well with lamb dishes.

COURGETTES AND ALMONDS

Dégorge courgettes to make them less watery. Sprinkle them with salt at the end of step 1, drain for 30 minutes, rinse and pat dry.

FRENCH BEANS WITH WATER CHESTNUTS

| 0.10 | £ | 245 cals |

Serves 1

100 g (4 oz) French beans

salt and freshly ground pepper

3 canned water chestnuts, drained

25 g (1 oz) butter or margarine

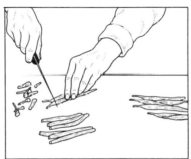

1 Top and tail the French beans. Cook in boiling salted water for about 3 minutes. Drain the beans and plunge into a bowl of cold water to set the colour and prevent any further cooking.

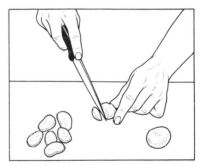

2 Meanwhile, slice the water chestnuts and set aside. Drain the beans. Melt the butter in a frying pan, add the French beans and cook, stirring, for 1–2 minutes. Stir in the water chestnuts and cook for a further minute, tossing the vegetables continuously. Season with salt and pepper and serve immediately.

3 To serve two: double the quantity of ingredients and follow the recipe above.

Menu Suggestion

Serve this unusual combination of vegetables with an oriental-style main course, or to add interest to plain roast or grilled meat.

FRENCH BEANS WITH WATER CHESTNUTS

It is possible to buy fresh water chestnuts from oriental specialist stores in some large cities, but canned water chestnuts are available in most supermarkets and make a perfectly acceptable substitute. They do not have much flavour, but are very crisp and crunchy, providing a good contrast to the tenderness of the beans. Water chestnuts are in fact a sweet root vegetable, and do not belong to the chestnut family at all.

SWISS FRIED POTATOES

| 0.35 | 🍴 | 566 cals |

Serves 1

30 ml (2 tbsp) butter

30 ml (2 tbsp) vegetable oil

200 g (7 oz) old potatoes, peeled

½ small onion, skinned and finely chopped

salt and freshly ground pepper

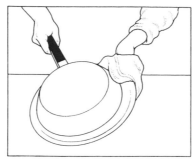

1 Melt half of the butter with half of the oil in a non-stick frying pan. Grate in the potatoes, then add the onion and salt and pepper to taste. Mix together. Press down well with a spatula.

2 Cover with a lid and cook over moderate heat for about 12 minutes, or until the potatoes are golden brown underneath.

3 Turn the potato cake out upside down on to a plate. Melt the remaining butter in the pan with the remaining oil.

4 Slide the potato cake back into the pan and cook for a further 12 minutes or until golden brown underneath. Slide out onto a warmed serving plate and serve immediately.

5 To serve two: double the quantity of ingredients and follow the recipe above.

Menu Suggestion
In Switzerland, these fried potatoes are often eaten as a snack, but they can equally well be served as a vegetable accompaniment to a steak, chop or sausages.

SWISS FRIED POTATOES

These delicious fried potatoes are a simplified version of the famous Swiss dish called *rösti*, which is made with chopped bacon and sometimes Gruyère or Emmental cheese. An alternative method of making this dish, which you might like to try, is to boil the potatoes in their skins for 15 minutes or until they are only just tender, then leave them until completely cold before peeling off the skins with your fingers. Grate the cold potato flesh, then cook as in the recipe above, but reduce the cooking time of the potato 'cake' to about 5 minutes on each side.

Swiss cooks maintain that *rösti* is best made with potatoes that have been cooked the day before. Waxy potatoes such as Estima, Maris Peer and Wilja are the best varieties for grating.

JAPANESE SALAD

| 0.20 | 122 cals |

Serves 1

50 g (2 oz) fresh spinach

salt

100 g (4 oz) white radish (see box)

1 medium carrot

30 ml (2 tbsp) shoyu

15 ml (1 tbsp) mirin

5 ml (1 tsp) vinegar

2.5 ml (½ tsp) caster sugar

10 ml (2 tsp) sesame seeds

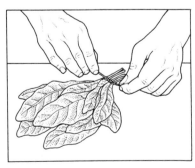

1 Tie the spinach leaves together around their stems, then plunge into a pan of boiling salted water. Bring back to the boil, then drain immediately. Cool, then pat dry with absorbent kitchen paper.

2 Peel the white radish and carrot, then grate them both coarsely into a bowl.

3 In a jug, mix together the shoyu, mirin, vinegar, sugar and salt to taste. Pour over the radish and carrot, then toss well until evenly mixed.

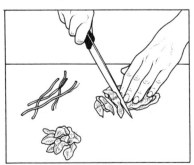

4 Cut the spinach leaves crossways into shreds, discarding the coarse stalks. Scatter the shreds over the salad. Toss gently to mix the spinach into the other ingredients, then sprinkle with the sesame seeds. Serve immediately.

5 To serve two: double the quantity of ingredients and follow the recipe above.

Menu Suggestion
Japanese Salad goes well with any oriental dish, or with plain roast or grilled meat.

JAPANESE SALAD
Look for white radish in large supermarkets by the name *mooli*, or in oriental stores under its Japanese name of *daikon*. It is a long white tapering root vegetable, which can be used raw in salads or cooked as a hot vegetable accompaniment. It is very crisp in texture, with a distinctive hot 'bite'. Shoyu is Japanese soy sauce, available from health food shops and oriental specialist stores. It is naturally fermented and milder in flavour than Chinese soy sauce. Mirin is sweetened sake or rice wine. It is available at Japanese food stores, but if you cannot obtain it, use sweet sherry instead.

WILTED SALAD

| 0.15 | 393 cals |

Serves 1

2 rashers of smoked streaky bacon

30 ml (2 tbsp) vegetable oil

1 small lettuce heart, leaves separated

few leaves of radicchio

2 spring onions, trimmed and finely chopped

15 ml (1 tbsp) wine vinegar

2.5 ml ($\frac{1}{2}$ tsp) caster sugar

salt and freshly ground pepper

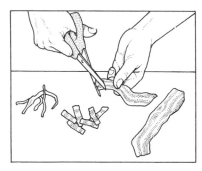

1 Cut the rind off the bacon with scissors, then snip the bacon into strips, discarding any bones.

2 Heat the oil in a heavy-based frying pan, add the bacon and fry over moderate heat, stirring constantly, until cooked.

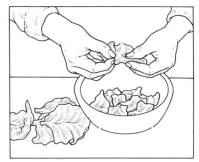

3 Meanwhile, tear the lettuce and radicchio leaves into a salad bowl. Sprinkle the spring onions over the leaves.

4 Remove the bacon from the pan with a slotted spoon and scatter over the salad. Add the wine vinegar and sugar to the residual oil in the pan and bring to the boil, stirring.

5 Pour the hot oil and vinegar dressing over the salad, sprinkle with salt and pepper to taste and toss gently to mix. Serve immediately.

6 To serve two: double the quantity of ingredients and follow the recipe above.

Menu Suggestion
Wilted Salad makes an unusual starter with hot garlic bread, or it can be served as a side salad for lunch or supper, with French bread and cheese.

Desserts and Baking

Treat yourself to
something sweet every
once in a while. When
you are eating alone,
nothing is more
guaranteed to cheer you
up—or make you feel
decidedly naughty!

SWEET SOUFFLÉ OMELETTE

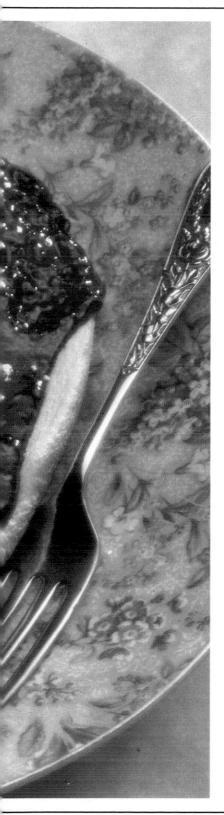

0.10 f 504 cals

Serves 1

2 eggs

10 ml (2 tsp) caster sugar

15 g (½ oz) butter or margarine

30 ml (2 tbsp) jam

30 ml (2 tbsp) icing sugar

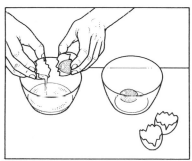

1 Separate the eggs, putting the whites in one bowl, the yolks in another. Add the sugar to the egg yolks and whisk well to mix. Whisk the egg whites until standing in stiff peaks.

2 Preheat the grill to hot. Melt the butter in a heavy-based omelette pan until foaming. Fold the egg whites quickly into the egg yolk mixture, then pour into the butter in the pan.

3 Cook over moderate heat for 2–3 minutes, without stirring, until the omelette is golden brown underneath.

4 Place the pan under the preheated grill and cook for 2–3 minutes more, until the top of the omelette is golden brown. At the same time, heat a metal skewer under the grill.

5 Warm the jam in a small pan. Slide the omelette on to a warmed plate. Spread with the jam, then fold the omelette over with the help of a fish slice or palette knife.

6 Sift the icing sugar thickly over the omelette, then carefully mark in a criss-cross pattern with the hot skewer. Serve immediately.

7 To serve two: double the quantity of ingredients and make a second omelette following the recipe above. Do not make a double quantity in the same pan.

Menu Suggestion
Sweet and rich, this soufflé omelette should be served on its own to be fully appreciated.

SWEET SOUFFLÉ OMELETTE

A soufflé omelette is just perfect for one person because it is so quick and easy to make. Each omelette has to be cooked separately, which makes it an impractical dessert to cook for more than one—or two people at the most. Take care not to stir the mixture in step 3 of the method or the omelette will scramble and not be as light and fluffy as it should be.

SABAYON

| 0.15* | £ £ | 232 cals |

*plus 1 hour chilling

Serves 2

50 g (2 oz) caster sugar

2 egg yolks

finely grated rind of $\frac{1}{2}$ lemon

juice of 1 lemon

30 ml (2 tbsp) rum, sherry or
   madeira

30 ml (2 tbsp) single cream

1 Put the sugar in a saucepan
with 60 ml (4 tbsp) water. Heat
gently until the sugar has
dissolved. Bring to the boil and
boil for 2–3 minutes, until syrupy.

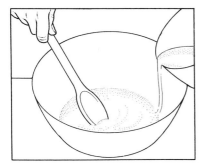

2 Put the egg yolks in a bowl and
beat lightly. Slowly pour on
the syrup, whisking constantly
until pale and thick.

3 Add the lemon rind, lemon
juice and rum, sherry or
madeira. Whisk for a further few
minutes, then stir in the cream.
Chill in the refrigerator for at least
1 hour before serving.

Menu Suggestion
Serve with sliced fresh fruits such
as melon, strawberries, grapes,
peaches or nectarines.

HOT CHOCOLATE SOUFFLÉS

| 0.30 | 🍴 £ | 666 cals |

Serves 2

15 g (½ oz) butter

40 g (1½ oz) plain chocolate

75 ml (5 tbsp) milk

10 ml (2 tsp) caster sugar

10 ml (2 tsp) plain flour

1 egg, separated

1 Use some of the butter to grease two 150 ml (¼ pint) soufflé dishes or ramekins.

2 Put the chocolate, 60 ml (4 tbsp) milk and the sugar in a small saucepan. Heat gently, stirring, until the chocolate is completely melted and the sugar dissolved.

3 Blend the remaining 15 ml (1 tbsp) milk with the flour in a small basin to make a smooth paste. Stir into the chocolate mixture.

4 Pour the mixture into the saucepan and bring to the boil. Cook for 2 minutes, stirring all the time. Stir in the remaining butter a little at a time, then remove the saucepan from the heat and leave the mixture to cool until lukewarm.

5 Beat in the egg yolk. Whisk the egg white until stiff and fold carefully into the chocolate mixture until evenly blended.

6 Turn the mixture into the soufflé dishes and bake in the oven at 200°C (400°F) mark 6 for about 15 minutes, until well risen and firm to the touch. Serve immediately.

Menu Suggestion

To make the soufflés look extra special, dust with a little icing sugar and serve with whipped or pouring cream.

HOT CHOCOLATE SOUFFLÉ

Take care when melting the chocolate in step 2 of the method. If the heat under the pan is too fierce, there is a danger that the chocolate will overcook and solidify into a lump. The addition of milk and sugar helps in this recipe, but if you are melting chocolate on its own it is always safer to melt it in a double boiler or heatproof bowl standing over a pan of simmering water. Do not over-stir the chocolate or this also may cause it to solidify. Wait until the chocolate has almost melted, then stir gently, once or twice at the most.

TANGERINE BRÛLÉES

0.40* £ £ 632 cals

* plus 5 hours chilling

Serves 2

150 ml (¼ pint) double cream

a few drops vanilla flavouring

2 egg yolks, size 6

45 ml (3 tbsp) caster sugar

1 tangerine, peeled and segmented

20 ml (4 tsp) orange-flavoured liqueur

1 Pour the cream into a small saucepan and heat until almost boiling, then remove from the heat. Add the vanilla flavouring.

2 In a medium bowl, beat together the egg yolks and 15 ml (1 tbsp) of the caster sugar until light in colour.

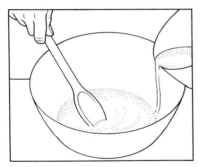

3 Pour the cream gradually on to the egg yolk and sugar mixture, stirring well.

4 Strain the mixture into the saucepan and cook, stirring over a gentle heat for about 10 minutes, or until the mixture coats the back of a spoon. Cover with greaseproof paper and allow to cool for 20 minutes.

5 Lay the segments of tangerine in the bottom of two 150 ml (¼ pint) ramekins and add 10 ml (2 tsp) liqueur to each one. Spoon the cooled custard mixture evenly into the ramekins, dividing it equally between them.

6 Cover with cling film then chill in the refrigerator for at least 3 hours or overnight.

7 Sprinkle the remaining sugar evenly over the top of each ramekin and put under a preheated hot grill for 2–3 minutes until the sugar turns to a caramel. Leave to cool for 15 minutes, then chill again for at least 2 hours.

Menu Suggestion

Serve for a special meal. When tangerines are not in season, substitute 1 small orange.

RASPBERRY CHEESECAKES

0.20* £ ✳ 815 cals

* plus 2 hours chilling

Serves 2

50 g (2 oz) cream cheese
5 ml (1 tsp) caster sugar
75 g (3 oz) fresh or frozen
  raspberries, thawed
100 ml (4 fl oz) double cream
15 g (½ oz) butter
2 digestive biscuits, finely crushed
whole raspberries, to decorate

1 In a small bowl, beat the cream cheese and 2.5 ml (½ tsp) of the sugar together until smooth. Add the raspberries and mix well.

2 Whip the cream until it just holds its shape, then fold into the cheese mixture until evenly incorporated.

3 Wet the insides of 2 ramekin dishes, to ensure that the mixture will turn out easily. Spoon in the cheese mixture, levelling it evenly.

4 Melt the butter in a saucepan and stir in the biscuits and remaining sugar.

5 Press the biscuit mixture on top of the cheese mixture and level the top. Chill in the refrigerator for at least 2 hours before serving.

6 To serve, loosen around the edges of the ramekins with a knife and turn the cheesecakes out on to 2 serving plates. Decorate with raspberries and serve chilled.

Menu Suggestion
Light and creamy, these cheesecakes make perfect summer desserts. Serve with crisp biscuits.

RASPBERRY CHEESECAKES

Soft cheeses labelled 'cream cheese' and 'full-fat soft cheese' contain 47 g fat per 100 g. Used in a cheesecake mixture such as this one they give a beautifully smooth texture and luscious, creamy flavour. If you are concerned about reducing fat in your diet, however, you can always use a soft cheese with a lower fat content. Curd cheese is made from semi-skimmed milk and has a medium fat content, but Quark has the lowest fat content of all the soft cheeses. Whipping cream has a butterfat content of 35–38 per cent, compared to double cream which has not less than 48 per cent butterfat. Whipping cream can be used in this recipe instead of double cream, with equally good results.

INDIVIDUAL PLUM PUDDINGS

1.30* £ £ ✳ 245 cals

*plus 24 hours standing, 1 hour cooling. At least 1 month maturing and 1 hour re-steaming

Makes 4

8 prunes, stoned and chopped

45 ml (3 tbsp) seedless raisins

45 ml (3 tbsp) currants

45 ml (3 tbsp) sultanas

12 whole blanched almonds, chopped

finely grated rind and juice of 1 tangerine

30 ml (2 tbsp) plain flour

2.5 ml ($\frac{1}{2}$ tsp) ground mixed spice

pinch of salt

30 ml (2 tbsp) fresh breadcrumbs

30 ml (2 tbsp) shredded suet

30 ml (2 tbsp) soft brown sugar

1 egg, size 4, beaten

30 ml (2 tbsp) brown ale

30 ml (2 tbsp) brandy, rum or sherry

sprigs of holly, to decorate

1 Place the dried fruits in a bowl with the nuts and tangerine rind and juice. Mix well.

2 In a separate bowl, sift together the flour, mixed spice and salt. Add the breadcrumbs, suet and sugar and mix well together.

3 Pour in the beaten egg and brown ale, beat well, then stir in the dried fruit mixture. Cover and leave in a cool place for 24 hours.

4 The next day, add the brandy, rum or sherry, stirring well. Butter 4 dariole moulds or ramekins and pack in the pudding mixture tightly.

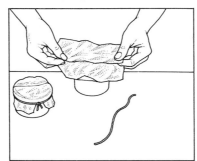

5 Cover the moulds with pleated greaseproof paper and foil and secure tightly with string.

6 Place the moulds in a large saucepan, then pour in enough boiling water to come halfway up the sides of the moulds. Bring to the boil and steam the puddings for about 1 hour, topping up with boiling water when necessary.

7 Remove the puddings from the pan and allow to cool completely for 1 hour.

8 Uncover the puddings, then re-cover in fresh greaseproof paper and foil. Store in a cool, dry place for at least 1 month (or up to 1 year) before serving.

9 To serve, steam in the same way for 1 hour. Turn out on to warmed individual serving plates and decorate each one with a sprig of holly.

Menu Suggestion
Serve on Christmas Day or for another celebration meal during the year. To make the pudding more festive, warm 30 ml (2 tbsp) brandy gently in a small saucepan, pour over the puddings and light carefully with a match. Serve with brandy or rum butter, whipped cream or custard.

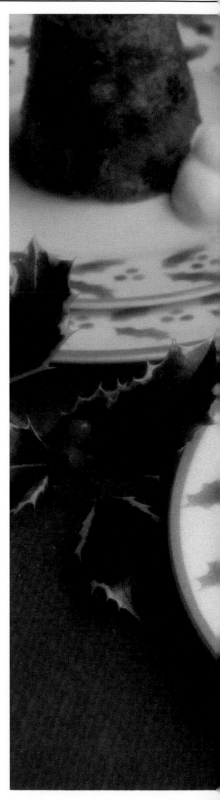

BOOZY BANANA

0.15	263 cals

Serves 1

15 g ($\frac{1}{2}$ oz) butter or margarine

15 ml (1 tbsp) soft brown sugar

30 ml (2 tbsp) freshly squeezed orange juice

30 ml (2 tbsp) sherry

1.25 ml ($\frac{1}{4}$ tsp) ground cinnamon

1 banana

orange twist, to decorate (optional)

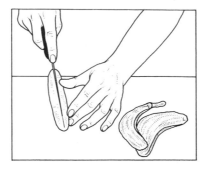

1 Melt the butter in a heavy-based frying pan. Add the remaining ingredients, except the banana. Heat gently, stirring, until the sugar has dissolved.

2 Peel the banana, then cut in half lengthways. Place in the pan and cook over gentle heat for about 10 minutes until tender. Baste the banana frequently with the sauce and turn the pieces over once during cooking. Serve hot, decorated with an orange twist, if liked.

3 To serve two: double the quantity of ingredients and follow the recipe above.

Menu Suggestion
Serve for a special dessert with chilled cream or vanilla ice cream. Alternatively, if you prefer the combination of sweet and tart flavours, serve with Greek yogurt, Quark or fromage blanc.

PLUM CROÛTE

0.25	🥄	324 cals

Serves 1

1 large slice of white bread

15 g ($\frac{1}{2}$ oz) butter or margarine, melted

2 ripe red plums, e.g., Victoria

25 g (1 oz) demerara sugar

1.25 ml ($\frac{1}{4}$ tsp) ground cinnamon

1 Cut the crusts off the slice of bread and discard. Brush both sides of the bread with the melted butter or margarine, making sure the bread is coated right to the edges.

2 Place the bread in an individual Yorkshire pudding tin, pressing it down well, but leaving the 4 corners protruding over the edge.

3 Bake the croûte in the oven at 200°C (400°F) mark 6 for 15–20 minutes until crisp and golden brown.

4 Meanwhile, halve and stone the plums, then place in a pan with the sugar and cinnamon. Sprinkle in 5–10 ml (1–2 tsp) water, then cook gently for about 5 minutes until the plums are tender and juicy but still retaining their shape.

5 When the croûte is cooked, transfer to a serving plate. Spoon the plums in the centre and serve immediately.

6 To serve two: double the quantity of ingredients and follow the recipe above.

Menu Suggestion
Serve with chilled cream or thick Greek yogurt for a sumptuously rich dessert.

CUT-AND-COME-AGAIN FRUIT CAKE

| 2.00* | £ | ✳ | 540–760 cals |

* plus 2 hours cooling and at least
1 day maturing

Makes one 20.5 cm (8 inch) cake

100 g (4 oz) plain flour

100 g (4 oz) self-raising flour

2.5 ml ($\frac{1}{2}$ tsp) ground nutmeg

2.5 ml ($\frac{1}{2}$ tsp) ground ginger

finely grated rind of $\frac{1}{2}$ lemon

50 g (2 oz) ground almonds

175 g (6 oz) butter or margarine

175 g (6 oz) caster sugar

4 eggs, beaten

350 g (12 oz) mixed dried fruit

100 g (4 oz) glacé cherries, halved

15 ml (1 tbsp) milk

25 g (1 oz) almonds, blanched and
slivered

1 Grease and line a 20.5 cm
(8 inch) round cake tin. Sift
the flours, nutmeg and ginger into
a bowl. Add the lemon rind and
almonds and stir well to mix.

2 In a separate bowl, cream the
butter and sugar together until
pale and fluffy. Add the eggs a
little at a time, beating well after
each addition. Fold in the flour
mixture with a metal spoon, then
the mixed dried fruit, halved glacé
cherries and milk.

3 Turn the mixture into the
prepared tin and make a slight
hollow in the centre. Scatter the
almonds over the top.

4 Bake the cake in the oven at
180°C (350°F) mark 4 for
1 hour, then lower the temperature
to 170°C (325°F) mark 3 and bake
for a further 30 minutes.

5 Remove from the oven and
allow to cool slightly for
15 minutes in the tin, before
removing to a wire rack to cool
completely for at least 2 hours.
Double wrap in greaseproof and
foil and place in an airtight tin.
Leave to mature for at least 1 day
before serving.

Menu Suggestion

This fruit cake improves with
keeping and should be stored for
at least 24 hours before being cut.
It is perfect for teatime snacks or if
visitors call unexpectedly, because
it will keep for several months if
wrapped in greaseproof paper and
foil and stored in a tin.

**CUT-AND-COME-AGAIN
FRUIT CAKE**

For a mild 'boozy' flavour to this
cake, prick the top of the cold
cake all over with a fine skewer
and slowly pour 30–45 ml
(2–3 tbsp) brandy over it before
wrapping and storing upside
down in a cake tin. If you are
planning to keep the cake for a
long time, this process can be
repeated at two-weekly intervals.

APPLE GINGERBREAD

1.30* £ ✳ 197 cals

* plus 1 hour cooling and 2–3 days maturing

Makes 12 slices

225 g (8 oz) plain flour

2.5 ml ($\frac{1}{2}$ tsp) salt

15 ml (1 tbsp) ground ginger

7.5 ml (1$\frac{1}{2}$ tsp) baking powder

7.5 ml (1$\frac{1}{2}$ tsp) bicarbonate of soda

100 g (4 oz) demerara sugar

75 g (3 oz) butter or margarine

75 g (3 oz) black treacle

75 g (3 oz) golden syrup

150 ml ($\frac{1}{4}$ pint) milk

1 egg, size 4, beaten

1 eating apple, cored and roughly chopped

1 Grease and line a 900 g (2 lb) loaf tin. Sift the plain flour into a large bowl with the salt, ginger, baking powder and bicarbonate of soda.

2 Put the sugar, butter, treacle and syrup in a saucepan and warm gently over low heat until melted and well blended. Do not allow the mixture to boil. Remove from the heat and leave to cool slightly, until you can hold your hand comfortably against the side of the pan.

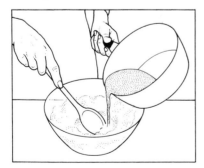

3 Mix in the milk and egg. Make a well in the centre of the dry ingredients, pour in the liquid and mix very thoroughly. Stir in the chopped apple.

4 Turn into the tin and bake in the oven at 170°C (325°F) mark 3 for about 1$\frac{1}{2}$ hours, or until firm to the touch.

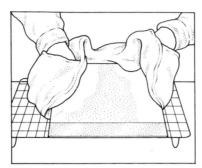

5 Turn out on to a wire rack to cool for at least 1 hour. Wrap in foil, then store in an airtight container for at least 2–3 days before eating.

Menu Suggestion
Gingerbread can be served plain, but it tastes even better when spread with butter. It is the perfect cake to include in a lunch box because it keeps so well, and it tastes particularly good with cheese and apple.

APPLE GINGERBREAD
Gingerbreads date back to medieval times, when they were made with honey rather than the black treacle and syrup used in modern recipes. In those days, gingerbread was made in slabs and sold at fairgrounds and markets, often with decorative patterns on the top made from real gold leaf or cloves with gilded heads—hence the expression 'the gilt on the gingerbread'.

   If you would prefer to make a smaller cake than the one here, use half the quantity of ingredients listed, with a size 6 egg. Bake in a deep 18 cm (7 inch) square tin for 1–1$\frac{1}{4}$ hours.

RICH CHOCOLATE CAKE

| 1.15 | £ £ ✳ | 692 cals |

✳ plus 1 hour cooling and 30 minutes
to set

Makes one 15 cm (6 inch) round cake

100 g (4 oz) plain flour

45 ml (3 tbsp) cocoa powder

2.5 ml ($\frac{1}{4}$ tsp) baking powder

large pinch bicarbonate of soda

large pinch salt

100 g (4 oz) plain chocolate

150 g (5 oz) butter or margarine

75 g (3 oz) light soft brown sugar

1 egg, size 4, beaten

75 ml (5 tbsp) natural yogurt

a few drops vanilla flavouring

150 g (5 oz) icing sugar

1 Grease and line a 15 cm
(6 inch) round cake tin with
greaseproof paper, leaving 2.5 cm
(1 inch) paper above the edge.

2 Sift the flour into a bowl with
15 ml (1 tbsp) of the cocoa
powder, the baking powder,
bicarbonate of soda and salt.

3 Break up 50 g (2 oz) of the
chocolate and put in a bowl
with 15 ml (1 tbsp) water. Place
over a pan of hot water and heat
gently, stirring, until melted.
Remove the bowl from the pan
and cool the chocolate.

4 Put 50 g (2 oz) of the butter in
a separate bowl. Add the brown
sugar and beat until fluffy. Beat in
the egg, then fold in the melted
chocolate and the sifted
ingredients.

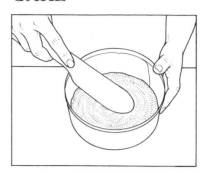

5 Turn the mixture into the
prepared tin and level the
surface. Bake in the oven at 190°C
(375°F) mark 5 for 45 minutes
until risen and firm to the touch.
Turn out on to a wire rack and
leave to cool for at least 1 hour.

6 Make the chocolate frosting.
Cream the remaining butter in
a bowl, sift in the icing sugar and
remaining cocoa powder and
cream again. Melt the remaining
chocolate in a small bowl over a
pan of hot water, leave to cool,
then beat into the creamed
mixture until evenly mixed.

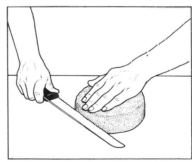

7 Split the cake into 2 halves.
Use half the frosting to
sandwich the cakes together and
smooth the remainder over the top
of the cake. Allow to set for at least
30 minutes before eating.

Menu Suggestion
This is just the cake to make for a
teatime treat when you have
visitors. It would also make a
delicious dessert, served with
whipped cream. Store wrapped
loosely in foil, in the refrigerator.

SHORTBREAD FINGERS

| 0.30* | £ | 83 cals |

* plus 35 minutes cooling

Makes about 14

125 g (4 oz) butter or margarine

50 g (2 oz) caster sugar

125 g (4 oz) plain flour

50 g (2 oz) ground rice

caster sugar, to dredge

1 In a bowl, cream the butter until soft. Add the caster sugar and beat until pale and fluffy.

2 Add the flour and ground rice and stir until the mixture binds together. Knead well to form a smooth dough.

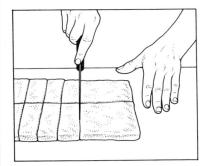

3 Roll out the dough on a lightly floured surface, to a square about 1 cm (½ inch) thick. Cut the square in half then cut each into fingers about 2 cm (¾ inch) wide.

4 Place the fingers well apart on a baking sheet and prick them with a fork. Bake in the oven at 180°C (350°F) mark 4 for about 15 minutes, or until pale golden and just firm to the touch.

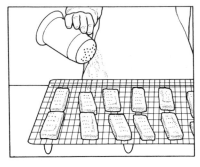

5 Transfer to a wire rack and leave to cool for 5 minutes. Dredge with caster sugar, then allow to cool completely for about 30 minutes. Store in an airtight tin for up to 1 week.

Menu Suggestion

Keep a tin of shortbread fingers for morning coffee and teatime treats, they are also useful to serve with creamy desserts and fruit salads. Or serve them with cheese, for an in-between-meal snack.

USEFUL INFORMATION
AND
BASIC RECIPES

Equipment and Gadgets

Equipping the kitchen for a small household is not the same as building a family kitchen. Not only are the quantities you cook smaller, your lifestyle is probably quite different too. So equipment that is ideal for a couple with three children could well be a white elephant to you living alone or as a twosome.

Life is always a compromise, and never more so than in equipping yourself to cook for a small household. You will need to draw a balance between economies of scale to suit the small meals normally required, and the extended facilities you may need occasionally for entertaining. Your own perception of your lifestyle will guide you when considering the relative importance of entertaining. But, certainly, nothing is worse than feeling you cannot have friends or family to a meal simply because you don't have the facilities to cook for, or seat, more than two. The sharing of a meal, however simple, is an important social bond from which you should beware of excluding yourself.

COOKERS

The centre of any kitchen must be the cooker. Even if you live in a bedsitter, you must have some means of cooking basic meals. You can wash up in the bathroom, work out ways of keeping food cool other than in a fridge, but without a cooker you would be restricted to eating raw foods.

Constraints of space and budget may force you to make other choices, but if money is no object and if you have the space, do consider a double oven. That will give you a small, economical oven that will cope with all the roasting and baking needed for one or two, plus a full size oven for when you

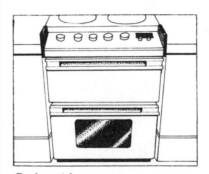

Cooker with two ovens

are entertaining. The second oven is also invaluable for keeping cooked foods hot while the rest of a meal is finished. And look for a large, powerful grill with an economy setting that allows you to heat just half at a time for cooking small quantities.

A standard hob has four rings, and many models provide an economy setting for small pans on at least one ring. If you can find a hob with two 'heat saver' rings it will be an advantage in a small household.

Beware of 'compact' cookers unless you are really pressed for space. They look deceptively like a standard cooker but the oven may well refuse to accommodate even a standard size roasting tin, and even if it has four rings on top you are unlikely to be able to get four pans on at the same time because the rings are so close together. If you choose a small cooker, a model with three rings, better spaced, is easier to use.

TABLE-TOP OVENS

A plug-in table-top oven is one answer in a really small kitchen, and it has the advantage of not needing a special power supply; a table-top oven is powered from an ordinary 13-amp socket. But they are limited in use, so if money is the constraint rather than space, a second hand conventional cooker is likely to be a better buy.

Table-top models are generally ovens only, with no hot plates. So you will need to buy and fit a hob of some description as well. The ovens are thermostatically controlled but settings are not usually marked in the same way as a conventional cooker and cooking generally takes longer; you will need to adjust normal recipes to suit. They are also not usually insulated to the same standard as a full size cooker, so the outside of the oven gets hot. This may be dangerous if it is not sited carefully.

For all the disadvantages, a table-top oven may be just the

Plug-in table-top oven

thing to suit *your* needs so do not discount the possibility, especially if you do most of your cooking by microwave and need conventional dry heat only occasionally.

MICROWAVE COOKERS

The microwave is probably more useful in a small household than anywhere else. It cooks small quantities of food superbly well and quickly. The time saving on larger quantities is relatively small.

To use a microwave cooker, though, you will have to abandon all you have ever learnt about cooking, and start from scratch learning new techniques. That may not be so daunting for a 20-year-old, but at 60 or so—which is a time of life when many people find themselves alone for the first time—it may be just another problem that is best avoided. For older people it is also worth remembering that the results of microwave cooking, however good and attractive, are different from the results of conventional

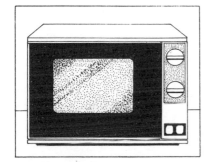

Microwave cooker

cooking. So there is an additional adjustment to make.

If you do decide to make the adjustment, savings in time, fuel and space are enormous. A microwave cooker runs off a 13-amp power socket, with no special wiring and can be placed on any sturdy table where there is sufficient space around it for ventilation. Cooking times are short, so the actual power consumed is usually a fraction of that which would be needed to cook a similar dish conventionally.

Unlike the table-top ovens mentioned before, a microwave cooker will cook most things that are otherwise cooked on a hob, so you don't need a hob as well, though an electric kettle is useful, as large quantities of water take a long time to boil by microwave. But you cannot fry or grill, so if those are favourite methods of cooking in your home, adjustments will have to be made.

Microwave cooking has lots of advantages if you live in a confined space. Cooking smells are much less than by conventional methods, and cooking can often be done in the serving dish, thus saving both washing up and storage of cooking utensils. If you live in a bedsitter or tiny flat, on a boat, or in some other unusual home you may be glad of all these points. And even if you live in an ordinary house you can still enjoy the same benefits. Another useful feature of the microwave is that the outside never becomes hot, so it is quite safe even for the elderly or disabled.

OTHER PLUG-IN COOKERS

There are various other electric cooking appliances that can either substitute for a proper cooker if you are in a bedsitter, or supplement it if you have a normal kitchen, giving big savings on fuel. **A multi-cooker,** sometimes known as an electric frying pan, is probably the most versatile. Made

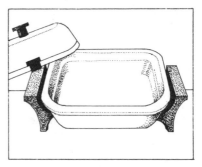

Multi-cooker or electric frying pan

like a large, usually rectangular, frying pan with a lid, a multi-cooker plugs into a socket and will substitute for many of the conventional cooker functions. It will not only fry but also casserole, steam, griddle, bake and even roast a small joint. The main constraint is the size of the pan, but it will always be large enough for two helpings and will often take more depending on the recipe. It will of course only cook one dish at a time, so if you are using it to cook the meat you will need a hob, or perhaps a microwave, to cook the vegetables or pudding.

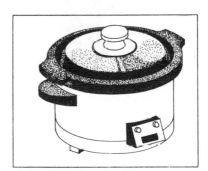

Slow cooker ideal for casseroles

The slow cooker is another popular gadget. Designed specifically for casseroles, it cooks at an exceptionally low temperature and is ideal for people who are out all day. You put all the ingredients for your dish in the slow cooker in the morning, switch it on and it cooks very slowly and gently all day, producing a beautifully tender, tasty stew by supper time. Because it operates on such low power it is cheap to run and, even better, it can not boil dry in the same way as a casserole left in the oven can.

Because of the low temperature, there are certain health hazards involved, but if you read the instruction book carefully these can be avoided. Follow the directions with care and you will find that the results are both excellent and economical.

Consider carefully the size of the slow cooker you buy, bearing in mind the size of your household. Consider too other options such as a removable inner dish that can double as a serving dish, saving washing up.

The slow cooker is not as versatile as some of the other appliances mentioned, but in a household where the chief cook is regularly out all day it can be worth its weight in gold.

Electric deep fat fryer

A deep fat fryer comes into a slightly different category. It is neither particularly economical to use nor expecially suitable for a small household. But it is nevertheless convenient and a gadget that any cook might consider buying. An electric deep fat fryer is fitted with a thermostat that keeps the oil at a fixed temperature, eliminating for ever soggy chips or fish that is golden and crisp on its batter-coated outside while the centre is still frozen.

In addition to the thermostat, most models have a filter in the lid which deals with the odours of frying. So if you love fried foods but can't stand the smell, this is the perfect answer.

For a small household, choose a small capacity fryer. Frying is quick, so cooking extra batches for guests is no problem.

REFRIGERATORS
Moving away from cooking to food storage, a refrigerator is usually one of the first considerations. The main thing to remember with a fridge is that it will be switched on permanently, using electricity. So it is important to choose a good quality one, that is properly insulated to use the minimum amount of electricity while maintaining a satisfactorily low temperature. Some mini-fridges that look about right for one person do not meet this criterion, so do check carefully what you are buying.

If you buy a refrigerator with a frozen food compartment, look for a 2- or 3-star marking just as you would for a bigger model.

Another point to check when buying a small fridge is that it will take the containers and foods that you are likely to put in it. For instance, is there a space for milk bottles, plus one that will take your favourite fruit juice jug? And is there sufficient depth on at least one shelf for a chicken?

How much refrigerator space you need will depend on your shopping visits. If you like to shop every day or several times a week, the smallest fridge you can find will be adequate. But if you are a once-a-weeker then a 140 litres (5 cu ft) capacity is unlikely to be too large for two people—it may even be a bit of a squeeze.

FREEZERS
A freezer is invaluable in a one- or two-person household (page 146), but a small one will do. A fridge-freezer is a popular choice as the combined models take up less space in a small kitchen, but a chest is cheaper to buy and more

Fridge-freezer takes up less space

economical to run. A chest freezer also gives more storage space for the size of the cabinet. However, if bending is a problem, then a small upright freezer in which you can see clearly what you have in each tray may be the solution.

Deciding which is the correct size is extremely difficult with freezers. Nearly everyone buying their first freezer soon wishes they had bought one a bit bigger. However, as a rough guide, it is usually sensible to allow 59 litres (2 cu ft) of storage space for each member of the family. Only if you buy whole carcasses of lamb or a side of pork are you likely to go beyond this.

For normal storage, freezers are designed with a thermostat that keeps the cabinet temperature at −18°C (0°F). This is the ideal temperature for storing frozen food. But if you are likely to be cooking lots of dishes for the freezer, or freezing fresh produce such as soft fruit or vegetables, you will need a model with a 'fast freeze' switch. This cuts out the

Chest freezer with 'fast-freeze'

thermostat and allows the temperature to go much lower. This means that the newly introduced food will freeze solid as quickly as possible without raising the temperature of what is already there. Look for a freezer with a 4-star symbol to be sure it is suitable for freezing fresh food as well as for storage.

Another factor that will influence your choice of freezer is where you intend to put it. Obviously, the kitchen is the most convenient place, but very often there simply isn't room. And even in a big kitchen, the warmth generated by central heating and cooking make it a less than ideal place to run a freezer economically. Although well insulated, a freezer is bound to have to work harder in a warm atmosphere. So a dry garage or outer passageway may be a more suitable choice. Otherwise there is nothing wrong with the landing or spare room, except that it will make a little noise when operating. But if the freezer is to be in an upstairs room (and this may be the kitchen in a flat, as well as a bedroom) check first that the floor will take the weight of the fully loaded cabinet.

DISHWASHERS

A dishwasher is probably not worth buying for one, but two healthy appetites will soon fill it. And if you do plenty of entertaining then you will certainly find it a welcome addition to the kitchen. But even in a small household, don't bother with a small model. Just because the sales leaflet says it will take 12 place settings, that doesn't mean it is built for 12 people. The occasional large bowl or oddly shaped dish will soon take up the space. Remember though that if you do decide to buy one you will also need to buy enough crockery so that you do not need to run the machine after each meal. Consider carefully, if space is a problem, where you will store the crockery.

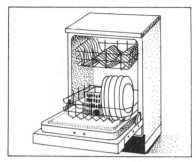

Make sure your crockery fits

When choosing a dishwasher, take along with you one of your large dinner plates to make sure it fits comfortably into the racks provided. The spaces between some racks, or the angle of the spikes, sometimes makes it difficult to accommodate a large plate that is not flat.

In a small household you will probably not want to run the dishwasher every day so a 'pre-wash' rinse facility is important. This rinses the plates when you put them in to remove the worst of the congealed food; it makes the final wash more thorough and also stops the half-full dishwasher becoming smelly. Also useful is an economy setting, so that if you run the occasional small load it is not so extravagant.

Most models plumb into the cold water supply and heat the water gradually to the selected temperature. This is the most effective way to wash, especially with proteins such as egg, which tend to become stuck on if plunged straight into hot water. Some manufacturers claim the machine can be run from the domestic hot water system up to about 55°C (131°F), but this temperature is lower than most people's hot water supply, so it doesn't really work. Better to face the cost and let the machine do the whole job.

The other main problem is caused by hard water. If you live in a hard water area it is important to choose a model with a water softener. Otherwise the

mechanisms will soon clog with lime. The softener operates on granular salt and it is wise to choose a model with a warning light that tells you when to fill up with salt—otherwise it is likely to be forgotten.

WASTE DISPOSALS

For a small household, do choose a small bin. Nothing is worse than the smell of rubbish left standing too long; it is much better that you be forced by the space available to empty it frequently. And keep your main dustbin well away from living areas, with the lid tightly on, to prevent smells wafting over from there.

The decision about electric waste disposal units is more a question of where you live than of how many in the house. If you live in the country and can use vegetable waste for compost, or if you have plenty of space outside for dustbins, then you may feel an electric unit is extravagant. But many single people or couples live in town flats where tramping a dustbin up and down stairs is one of the most unpleasant chores of the week. In this situation a sink

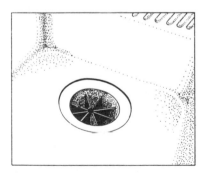

Sink waste disposal unit

disposal unit is well worth considering. It will eat up all vegetable peelings, kitchen scraps and small bones, leaving you only with things like packaging and bottles for the bin.

SAUCEPANS

On the whole, food cooks better if it just fits comfortably into the pan. A small amount of food in the bottom of a big pan is more likely to burn and will not cook so evenly as it would in the correct size pan. So for a small household choose small pans. But you will need a big saucepan and casserole for when visitors come.

Small pans will be more useful

Don't assume you have to buy a set of saucepans. Odd ones, chosen each for its special purpose, are likely to be more useful, even though they may not stack easily for storage or look so pretty on open shelves. But the first consideration must always be the fuel you cook on. For an electric hob it is important to choose pans with a heavy base, otherwise they will buckle in no time. With a gas hob you can get away with more lightweight utensils. If you have a ceramic hob, be guided by the manufacturer's recommendations for the best type of pans to use.

If you have a dishwasher, check that any new pans you buy are suitable for washing in it. It is always a pity when the machine will cope with the plates but leaves you with the horrible pans.

KETTLES

Although more expensive, electric kettles are more popular than those you place on the hob. If your hob is electric, an electric kettle is essential as it is virtually impossible to buy a non-electric one with a sufficiently heavy base.

Kettle with automatic cut-out

Look for a kettle with an automatic cut out so that it cannot boil dry. If you are a one-cupper, consider the jug type which will boil much smaller quantities than a standard kettle.

KNIVES

The size of your household makes no difference to your need for knives. You still cannot do without a collection of different shapes and sizes, kept really sharp. These are

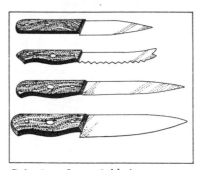

Selection of essential knives

the essential ones: a small pointed one for paring vegetables, a serrated one for tomatoes and citrus fruits, a middle-sized one for slicing and filleting, and a big heavy one for chopping.

The old-fashioned carbon steel blades are easiest to keep sharp, but they are difficult to keep clean. They should be wiped and dried immediately after use and should never be left in water or they will rust. They certainly are not dishwasher-proof. If you have a set of which some are used only occasionally, keep those lightly

oiled with cooking oil. From time to time all your knives will need cleaning thoroughly. A hard scrub with a green scouring pad dipped in neat washing up liquid should remove all stains and rust spots and bring them up shining again.

Stainless steel knives are much less trouble, but do not always have a good edge. Hollow ground knives tend to stay sharp longest, and if you really have difficulty look for a professional knife sharpener. Once they have been done professionally, your knives will usually last much longer than if you struggle yourself.

MIXERS, FOOD PROCESSORS AND BLENDERS

The full-sized free-standing mixer is really designed for people who do a lot of baking. It creams, whisks, mixes and kneads in quite large quantities, which may not be suitable when you are cooking for one or two. Of course it also does all sorts of other things, from liquidising soups and pâtés to making cream or sausages. Attachments for these functions, plus slicers and shredders, sieves, knife sharpeners and can openers make it a very versatile machine. But its prime purpose is in beating and creaming, so unless you like to batch bake for the freezer (page 148) you will not get as much use out of it as a large family might.

A food processor is more compact, cheaper and probably more versatile for a one-or-two

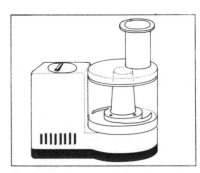

Food processor

person household. With it you can chop, slice and purée, you can cream small quantities for a sandwich cake, make lovely light pastry and even knead bread dough in small quantities. A few processors have a whisk attachment for use with egg whites and cream but this is not usually very powerful, and the limited space in the enclosed bowl means you can only whisk small quantities. So you will probably need to back up a food processor with a hand-held electric whisk.

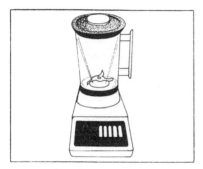

Electric blender

A blender makes slightly smoother soups and purées than a food processor, but the difference is marginal. Of course a blender is much cheaper than a food processor, so if you only want a machine for the purpose of liquidising, then you may prefer it. But its uses are strictly limited.

SMALL GADGETS

The number of small gadgets available for kitchen use is endless. We all know someone who swears by a gadget that we wouldn't give house room to. But there are certain old favourites that are genuinely useful.

A toaster is one. Certainly good toast can be made under the grill. But heating an electric grill for toast is very wasteful on fuel. The grill must be thoroughly hot before you start to cook, which involves several minutes of preheating. A gas grill is more efficient in this respect, but neither type self-ejects like a

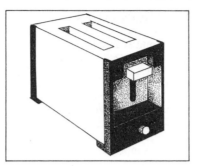

Toaster with an economy setting

toaster and a fair number of rounds get forgotten and burnt.

For one or two people, look for a toaster with an economy setting. This will allow you to cook one slice of toast without heating both slots. The elements are very small, and the bread is held very close to the heat so there is no waste.

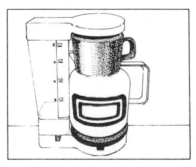

Electric filter coffee maker

An electric filter coffee maker is also a good investment if you like good coffee. It not only makes the coffee without your constant supervision, but it keeps it hot too, at a temperature that does not ruin the flavour.

Most models have a widely varying capacity, so that even the largest can be used to make only one or two cups when you wish. If buying a machine with a large capacity, look for one that has an adjustment for the rate of water flow depending on how many cups you are making. If the machine is set to make, eight cups, for example, the water will flow too fast to make two cups satisfactorily.

A few very small coffee makers are available, to make one or two individual cups rather than a jug full. Some are attached to an alarm clock—ideal for the early morning rush.

Healthy Eating

Eating healthily is fun. To eat well you need a widely varied diet, which can give you a lot of pleasure. And if you are cooking for one or two you don't have to take into account the faddy tastes of a whole family—you are free to experiment to your heart's content.

CARBOHYDRATES

Carbohydrate, in the form of starch and sugars found in unrefined cereals, fruits and vegetables (including pulses) is an essential source of energy and should form 55–60 per cent of our total energy intake. Unrefined carbohydrates such as wholegrain cereals, wholemeal flour, brown rice, vegetables and fruit, are an important source of fibre.

Dietary fibre is made up of cellulose, demicellulose, pectins, gums and lignin; it is not a single substance. Fibre passes through the intestines just about intact. It absorbs water like a sponge which enables the smooth passage of waste products and prevents constipation. Western diet is deficient in fibre, and it is recommended that we increase our fibre intake to 30 grams per day by increasing our 'whole foods', that is unrefined foods, and by eating more fruit and vegetables.

Concentrated refined carbohydrate foods made with white flour—such as cakes, biscuits, pastries—are easily digested and a popular form of snack for a quick energy boost. But because they are so easy to digest we quickly become hungry again afterwards.

It therefore makes more sense to eat them in an unrefined form, using wholegrain flour and cereals. Wholegrain flours and cereals are an important source of carbohydrate, essential for energy. The protein present needs to be complemented by eating cereal

Carbohydrate-containing foods

with legumes, pulses, nuts or milk products. Wholegrain cereals are rich in B vitamins, and vitamin E. They also provide calcium, iron, zinc and potassium, amongst other minerals. In this form they pass more slowly and effectively through the digestive tract, yielding up a variety of nutrients. Because the fibre is not removed they also have the advantage of adding dietary bulk, preventing or limiting many bowel related diseases.

PROTEIN

Protein is the main body building food, essential for growth and repair of tissues. Seventy-five per cent of our body's solid mass is made up of protein, and it is important to eat some protein food every day to replace that used up by everyday life.

Remember that protein does not just mean expensive meat.

Foods high in protein

Protein is present in high quantities in fish, poultry, eggs, milk and milk products like cheese and yogurt. It is also present in cereals, bean curd (tofu), pulses (beans and lentils), nuts and seeds. Vegetable (plant) sources of protein, such as those mentioned above, have to be eaten in a mixture of two from each group (for example, cereals and beans) to complement the different proteins present in each. The complemented proteins make them every bit as good as animal proteins.

The more you ring the changes

between these foods, the healthier you will be, so long as you eat a good portion of one of them every day. As a general guide, most adults need about 50 g (2 oz) of protein each day —a very small amount when you think of the steaks and chops we generally serve ourselves. Children, adolescents and pregnant women's needs will vary from this.

FATS

Fats provide insulation to keep us warm, protection against knocks for our internal organs, and energy; weight for weight they provide twice as much energy as protein or carbohydrate. Fats are a source of fat soluble vitamins A, D, E, and K, as well as essential fatty acids. They also provide a useful function in making other foods more appetising. Butter or margarine makes bread tastier, dripping juices improve the flavour of roast meat, a dressing improves salad. But beware of excess, especially the hard 'saturated' fats (see Cholesterol-Lowering Diet —page 140).

It is estimated by nutritionists that our daily diet should include a minimum of 10 per cent fats. But the average amount for the Western world is over 40 per cent, so the experts are recommending that we should reduce our intake to 30–35 per cent. This isn't necessarily easy, since so many fats are 'invisible' in foods such as avocados and nuts as well as pastries. If you have a specific medical condition that demands

Foods high in 'invisible fats'

Low fat spread, cheese and milk

severe reduction of fat you will simply have to learn to cook differently. But for most people it helps if you use skimmed milk, low-fat cheese such as cottage, and low-fat spreads as a substitute for butter. Eat more fresh fruit and vegetables when you want snacks, and avoid nuts, crisps and chocolates. Grill rather than fry where possible, and if you do fry use a light oil such as sunflower or safflower rather than lard or butter. In general, be careful how much you eat of pastry and cakes, and salad dressings and sauces made with oil or butter.

VITAMINS

Vitamins are found, in varying amounts, in all foods.

Vitamin D is particularly important to the growth and formation of bones because it helps the absorption of calcium from the intestine and controls the amount that is retained. So while it is especially important for children (remember all that cod liver oil poured down you as a child?) it is also vital for the elderly, whose bones tend to become brittle and break easily, and for pregnant women.

Vitamin D comes mostly from exposure of our skin to sunlight. This is fine in summer, but in winter when sunlight is scarce, or if you are housebound, you need to supplement it from food sources.

The main food source of vitamin D are oily fish such as

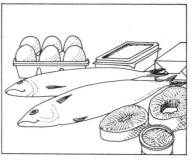

Food high in vitamin D

mackerel, herring, salmon and tuna; margarine, which is fortified with vitamin D by law; eggs and butter. Margarine, butter and other dairy products and eggs are also good sources of vitamin A, along with liver and kidney and the dark green and yellow vegetables such as spinach and carrots.

Vitamin C is another element that occurs only in a limited range of foods. This vitamin is necessary to keep the connective tissue between cells healthy. Deficiency quickly results in bleeding, especially of the gums, and wounds heal more slowly. Severe lack of vitamin C results in scurvy and finally death. Fresh vegetables

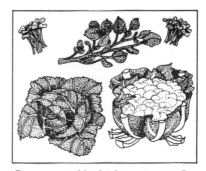

Green vegetables high in vitamin C

and fruit are the main sources of vitamin C, freshness being the key. Long storage and poor preparation or cooking destroy the vitamin content, so buy frequently, cook quickly and lightly, use vegetable cooking water to make sauces, and eat raw fruits and salads regularly.

Vitamin E appears to be essential for muscular health and blood circulation, though not a great deal is known about it. Elderly people in particular would do well to make sure they get a good supply—it is readily available in the form of wheatgerm, vegetable oils, wholemeal bread, egg yolks, green vegetables and nuts.

Vitamin A is necessary for good vision in dim light, as well as for the maintenance of healthy skin and mucus membranes. The richest sources are oily fish, like mackerel, offal, dairy produce and eggs. Carrots, red peppers, pumpkin and sweetcorn, and dark green vegetables like spinach, broccoli, mustard cress and avocados, are also good sources.

The Vitamin B group is a very complex group of substances needed for all sorts of body functions, including functioning of the nervous system, production of a healthy blood supply and utilisation of other nutrients. Many B vitamins are involved in the production of energy from carbohydrates. As illustrations of its complexity, it has been suggested that some of the problems of old age, such as memory loss and at its extreme senile dementia, may be at least partly attributable to B group deficiencies; similarly, symptoms of lethargy known as 'jet lag' or 'going off clock' can also be corrected with supplementary doses from the vitamin B group.

Important food sources for the B group of vitamins are milk,

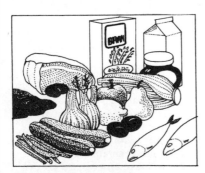

Foods high in vitamin B

offal, meat, fish, eggs, vegetables and fruit, wholegrain cereal and bread, fortified breakfast cereals and yeast extract—in fact a widely varied diet.

B vitamins such as thiamin (B_1) are easily destroyed by cooking methods such as excessive boiling of vegetables and the addition of bicarbonate of soda to the cooking water.

Vitamin K is necessary for the normal clotting of blood. It is present in many vegetables and can also be synthesised within our bodies by our intestinal bacteria. Dietary deficiencies are therefore unlikely.

Excessive intakes of water soluble vitamins (i.e., B and C) either from vitamin pills or from an unusual diet, have very little effect and are mostly excreted in the urine. Vitamins A, D, E and K are fat soluble, so that excessive intake accumulates in the body and can be dangerous. However, excesses are unlikely if you eat a normal diet.

MINERALS

Minerals cannot be manufactured by the body and so have to be obtained from food sources. There are about fifteen of them known to be essential, though mainly in very small amounts. The main functions of minerals are as constituents of bones and teeth, as soluble salts which control the composition of body fluids and cells, and as additions to other foods for the release and utilisation of energy.

Iron is probably the most commonly talked about mineral. This helps in the formation of red blood cells and a shortage means fewer and smaller cells—resulting in an inadequate supply of oxygen round the body causing weakness, dizziness and a constant feeling of lethargy. An 'iron tonic' is the traditional, self-prescribed medicine for anyone feeling really run down, but iron is found in meat, offal (especially liver), canned sardines, wholegrain

Foods high in iron

cereals, apricots, potatoes, watercress, treacle, curry powder and baked beans plus many other foods. So a varied diet should provide enough for normal needs. Vitamin C-containing foods eaten at the same time make non-meat sources of iron more available.

Calcium is the most abundant mineral in the body, giving bones and teeth their structure and strength. Calcium is also essential for the contraction of muscles for nerve function and for the normal clotting of blood. In children, calcium deficiencies result in stunted growth and in rickets; in old people it shows as decalcified, brittle bones.

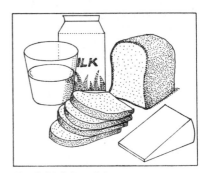

Foods high in calcium

The main food sources of calcium are milk, cheese, bread and green vegetables, so it is important to include these in your diet. But unfortunately the calcium cannot be absorbed without adequate amounts of vitamin D, so the two must go side by side (although not necessarily at the same meal).

Phosphorus is the second most abundant mineral in the body, with a wide variety of functions, but since it is in nearly all foods, deficiencies are virtually unknown. **Magnesium** is likewise widespread, deficiencies usually result from a prolonged bout of diarrhoea rather than low intake. **Sulphur,** too, is present in all protein foods so if you eat those you will have enough of the mineral too.

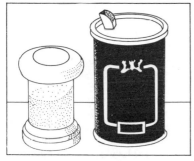

Low sodium salts

Sodium and potassium are largely obtained from the salt we add to food during cooking and at table. Potassium is also found in animal products, wholegrain cereals, pulses and legumes. Although they play an important part in nerve function and in maintaining the body's water balance, we are inclined to take too much rather than too little because of acquired tastes for salty food. **Zinc** is the remaining important mineral, and is easily lost during food processing. It is essential for normal growth and development, healthy skin and hair and wound healing. It is found in meat, seafood, wholegrains and nuts.

Keep it mixed
A quick glance at the 'food sources' mentioned under the various headings above will confirm that practically all foods contain something of value, and nothing contains all we need. So the secret of healthy eating is to plan your meals to take in as wide a variety of foods as possible.

You don't need to eat a perfectly balanced diet every day. The odd junk meal or day of snacks will even itself out over a week of varied eating.

Living alone, or in a small household of only two, some people despair at always having to buy in such small quantities and increasingly turn to a limited range of convenient dishes. To combat this, try to develop a sense of the fun of food. Use your solitude as an opportunity to try new foods—after all, if they don't turn out quite as you expected there is no one else to grumble. There is an art in shopping for small numbers too, mainly involving buying loose foods instead of pre-packed goods which tend to be in quantities more suitable for a family. For health, go for fresh or frozen foods, keeping canned and processed foods just for back-up, when you get caught unable to go out shopping.

Special diets
Special diets may present problems. If you are advised to follow one, either to treat a disorder such as diabetes or as a preventive measure against future illness, do stick to it as closely as possible. If your doctor's advice is too general to be really useful, ask him to recommend a dietician or enquire about any specialist organisation that deals with your condition. There are many organisations that can give detailed advice on particular problems and supply interesting and appropriate recipes.

SLIMMING
A slimming diet is something that many people embark upon without specialist advice. They may follow advice in a newspaper or magazine, or just go on their own ideas. But whatever the basis for a slimming diet, it is important to maintain a balance of nutrients just as in a normal diet. The trick is in simply eating less.

To really control the amount they eat, most people use a calorie-counting diet. Calories are the units used to measure the energy value of food. Counting them involves using a chart to establish the calorific value of each food — charts and books are published by many organisations and are easy to buy in a large newsagents or book

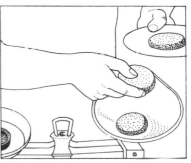

Weighing out each portion of food

sellers—and weighing each portion of food you eat.

Most women need about 1200 calories a day to lose weight and still stay healthy; men need about 1700. If you cut down more than this, don't go below 1000 calories for women or 1400 for men without medical advice. (These figures are different for elderly people or those with very active jobs. If you fall into either category, take specialist advice.)

With this type of diet it is important to be totally honest with yourself, and include in your count every little snack right through the day. But it does have the advantage that no foods are totally forbidden; if you choose to blow your ration one day on a cream bun and a large gin and tonic, for example, that's alright once in a while. It isn't possible to go for long like that, though, as you will be too hungry and will search out the more satisfying foods.

Another popular method of slimming is by a carbohydrate-controlled diet.

There is, however, a danger with a carbohydrate-controlled

DAILY FOOD INTAKE

A woman on 1200 calories per day should have:

6 portions of unrefined carbohydrate e.g.,
1 portion	= 1 slice wholemeal bread
or	= 1 medium potato
or	= 1 Weetabix or Shredded Wheat
or	= 50 g (2 oz) brown rice or wholemeal pasta (cooked)

3 portions of fresh fruit e.g.,
1 portion	= 1 apple
or	= 1 orange

3 portions of protein e.g.,
1 portion	= 50–75 g (2–3 oz) meat (lean) or oily fish
or	= 100 g (4 oz) chicken (no skin)
or	= 175 g (6 oz) fish (white)
or	= 1 egg
or	= 175 g (6 oz) legumes or pulses (cooked)
or	= 50 g (2 oz) hard cheese or 100 g (4 oz) cottage cheese

and

	400 ml (⅔ pint) semi-skimmed milk
or	200 ml (⅓ pint) whole milk per day
or	600 ml (1 pint) skimmed milk

and

	15 g (½ oz) margarine or butter
or	15 ml (1 tbsp) polyunsaturated oil
or	25 g (1 oz) low-fat spread

As many vegetables as liked

No added sugar should be used at all and if food requires sweetening, then a sweetener should be used.

diet. Even on a reducing diet, 55–60 per cent of energy must come from carbohydrates. If insufficient energy is available from carbohydrates, the body will use protein as an energy source, possibly risking a protein deficiency. Over a long, sustained slimming period, a calorie-counting diet is both safer and more likely to succeed.

CHOLESTEROL-LOWERING DIET

There has been a lot of interest recently in the possibility of reducing the amount of coronary heart disease in our society by adjusting our diet. Those who know they suffer from heart disease will be given dietary guidance by their doctors, but we can all reduce the risk of diet-induced heart disease by eating a low cholesterol diet.

Cholesterol is a fatty substance which is present in all human tissue, including blood. It performs essential functions in the body, but it also contributes to the thickening of the artery walls that causes much heart disease. Cholesterol either comes directly from cholesterol-rich

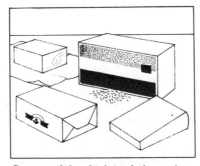

Saturated fats high in cholesterol

foods —meat, egg yolks, offal, butter, cream —or it is manufactured in the body. Saturated fats are, generally speaking, animal fats such as lard, suet, mutton fat, butter and hard cheese; hard vegetable fats, such as hard margarine, are also included in this category, as are coconut and palm oil. Plants contain no cholesterol, so fruits, vegetables and vegetable oils are cholesterol free.

To reduce cholesterol in the diet, reduce the amount of saturated fats you eat. They are the hard fats that are solid at room temperature. Surprisingly, it also helps to *add* polyunsaturated fats —these are the very soft fats, mostly of vegetable origin, such as corn, sunflower and safflower seed and soya bean oil. Polyunsaturated fats help reduce the risk of heart disease firstly by reducing blood cholesterol levels and secondly by reducing the risk of blood clotting, or thrombosis.

In practice, eating a cholesterol-lowering diet means avoiding hard animal fats and also cream, full-fat cheese and butter. Eat chicken, veal and fish in preference to pork, beef or lamb and cut off all visible fat from meat. You should also restrict your intake of egg yolks to 4–5 a week and offal to once a

Food for a low-cholesterol diet

week. Substitute low-fat yogurt, cottage cheese and skimmed milk for dairy produce and eat as much as you like in the way of fruit, vegetables and cereals.

To increase your intake of

BASIC GUIDELINES FOR HEALTHY EATING

Obviously no-one needs to eat a perfectly balanced diet every day. The odd junk meal or day of snacks will even itself out over a week of varied eating. Fresh foods which have not undergone any processing are obviously better than packaged versions, but make sure that they really are fresh. Canned, dried and frozen foods can be just as good as fresh.

Read the list of ingredients on manufactured food packaging, so you can avoid those foods containing excessive amounts of sugar, salt or undesirable additives such as colouring or preservatives.

For most people a healthy diet means
- Eating less fat. Aim to cut total fat intake by at least a quarter and saturated fat by half.
- Eating less sugar. Aim to cut sugar intake by at least half.
- Eating less salt.
- Eating more dietary fibre (roughage).

Aim towards
- Being the correct weight for your height and bone structure.
- Drinking in moderation.
- Not smoking.

Foods to eat less of
- Fatty meats such as pork, lamb, beef and bacon. Meat products such as pies, sausages, pâtés, burgers. Cooked and cured meats such as salami, corned beef, luncheon meat.

- Dairy foods such as butter, full fat milk and cheese, cream, ice cream.
- Hard margarines, dripping, lard and other animal shortenings.
- Cakes, biscuits and pastries. Refined and sweetened breakfast cereals, ready-made desserts, confectionery, soft drinks, snacks such as crisps and salted nuts.
- Cut down the amount of sugar added to food and drinks and reduce the number of snacks between meals.
- Cut down the amount of salt added to foods.
- Limit the number of egg yolks consumed to only three to five a week.

Foods to eat more of
- Poultry such as chicken and turkey, game, rabbit (all low in saturated fat) and offal. Lean cuts of other meats with visible fat trimmed off.
- Fish, both white and oily types. The latter contains a type of fatty acid which may actually protect against heart disease. Eat at least one oily fish meal each week (mackerel, herring, sardine).
- Low fat dairy foods such as skimmed or semi-skimmed milk (the latter is virtually indistinguishable from full fat milk), low or medium fat cheese and low fat yogurt.
- Fresh fruit and vegetables, including potatoes. Leave skins on and eat raw wherever possible to retain maximum nutrients.

- Unrefined cereal products, such as wholemeal flour and bread and wholegrain breakfast cereals.
- Pulses, beans, rice, pasta and noodles, especially the unrefined varieties.
- Soft margarine labelled 'high in polyunsaturates' which is relatively low in saturated fats. Pure vegetable oils, such as sunflower, soya, safflower corn and olive. Use these alternatives to other fats like butter and hard margarines, but still try and cut down on them.

Meal planning
Aim to eat daily:
- Bread and cereals including rice and pasta: 4 servings or more.
- Vegetables and fruit: 4 servings or more, including at least one raw.
- Meat, offal, poultry, fish, eggs, cheese or pulses: 1–2 servings, vary the choice throughout the week and, eat lean meats and low fat cheeses.
- Milk: children and adolescents, 568 ml (1 pint); adults, 300 ml ($\frac{1}{2}$ pint). Apart from infants, switch to semi or skimmed milk.
- Up to 15–25 g ($\frac{1}{2}$–1 oz) of butter, margarine or cooking oils: remember part of this intake will come from the preparation of other foods. Also, do not forget to take account of the hidden fats in baked goods, such as cakes, pies and biscuits.

polyunsaturates, substitute polyunsaturated margarine for butter, and use corn, soya, sunflower or safflower oil instead of hard fats.

VEGETARIAN DIETS
If you feel, for health or aesthetic reasons, that you should avoid meat in your diet, it is perfectly possible to eat well and be healthy.

Vegetable protein is adequate, but the diet needs balancing carefully. Before switching from

one to the other, therefore, do go into the subject.

Ingredients

Don't be shy about buying in small quantities. If two apples are what you want, ask for them. Likewise there is no shame in buying one chop or 100 g (4 oz) mince. Family units are becoming progressively smaller than they have traditionally been, and suppliers are prepared to market their goods accordingly.

When shopping for one or two you will find that some supermarkets are unsuitable. If they sell only prepackaged produce, especially vegetables and meat, the packs may be too large for your convenience, being designed for families. So choose your retailer. Many supermarkets now favour loose produce, so you can hand select exactly what you want or talk to a butcher behind the meat counter. This system has the added advantage that you need buy only perfect produce. Otherwise get to know your local specialist stores for personal service.

A good storecupboard comes close behind the fresh food supply in making a happy success of your cooking. A good selection of canned and packaged foods in stock is by far the easiest way of adding variety to your diet of fresh foods. Most canned foods are available in small sizes. These may cost more weight for weight than the larger ones, but an economy size is false economy if you end up refrigerating leftovers and then throwing them out. When buying frozen foods, look for loose packs so you can take a little out and reseal the pack; solid packs are very difficult to break up.

Most storecupboard foods keep well, so you don't need to limit what you buy. Just make sure you keep them in a cool, dry cupboard and use them in rotation. It is a good idea to mark cans and packets with the date when you buy them (see chart on page 143 for storage times).

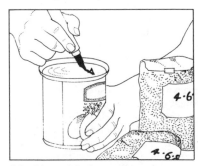

Marking with the purchase date

Go through the cupboard regularly, say every six months, and invent ways to use up anything that is nearing the end of its shelf life. This way you can give yourself an unexpected treat. For instance, many single people won't bake a cake just for themselves, but the decision to use up a packet of flour before it deteriorates may result not only in a fresh, home-made chocolate cake but in an invitation to friends to come and help you eat it.

DRY INGREDIENTS

Packaged dry ingredients can be kept quite safely in the original packet until opened, after which the contents should be transferred

Transfer dry food to a storage jar

to a storage jar with a well-fitting lid. Really airtight lids are essential only for strong-smelling foods like coffee, herbs and spices, which lose their aroma and flavour when exposed to the air, and for things like salt and baking powder which absorb moisture easily and become caked.

Cereal products such as flour and rice keep well if the cupboard is dry, but watch out for insect or mouse damage. Affected foods should be thrown out at once and the stock in that cupboard checked to make sure the damage goes no further. Don't mix fresh flour with the remains of an old packet in your storage jar as this encourages rancidity. Finish off the old first and wash out the jar thoroughly before you empty in the new packet. The high fat content of wholemeal flour and oatmeal mean they do not keep as long as other cereals, so use them up quickly.

Dried fruits need cool, dry storage as they are liable to ferment in damp conditions and shrink in a warm atmosphere. Nuts should be used up quickly as their fat content makes them liable to go rancid.

PRESERVES

Jams and marmalades that are sealed properly and stored in a cool dry place should keep indefinitely, but if mould growth develops there is no need to waste the whole jar. Scrape off the

Scraping off the mould from jam

mould and use up the rest of the jam as quickly as possible. If jams or preserves have fermented, however, throw away the whole jar. Syrups and honey will crystallise if kept too long, but are still quite safe and can be used for sweetening even if they will not spread.

CANNED INGREDIENTS

Canned fish and meat, with the exception of fish in tomato sauce, are safe to keep for several years, provided the cans remain in good condition. Ham does not keep quite so well; cans weighing less than 900 g (2 lb) will have been sterilised and are safe for 2–3 years, but large canned hams will only have been pasteurised and should be kept in the refrigerator for not more than 6 months.

Canned fruit is best used within

a year as the contents may deteriorate in colour after this time, although the food value is not altered. Condensed milk will begin to discolour after 6–9 months. Dried full–cream milk will keep for a few weeks after opening but then tends to go rancid, so the skimmed milks are probably a better buy for occasional use.

Always discard any cans that have 'blown'—recognisable by bulging ends and leaking or rusty seams.

WINE

Wine for cooking or occasional drinking used to be a problem in small households. Half bottles have always been available but are prohibitively expensive compared with full bottle prices. Now, however, cans and mini–bottles are available, containing about two glasses. Even better are wine

Wine keeps well in wine boxes

boxes. These are usually reasonable quality blended wines and the contents really do keep after opening because the air cannot get to them. Oxidation is the main reason for the deterioration of ordinary wines once opened, and in a box this cannot happen. You can take a glass or a spoonful at will with no waste.

Finally, there are advantages to shopping in small quantities as well as disadvantages, cost being the main one. For a special occasion you may be able to afford fillet steak or a rack of lamb for two, where buying for a family of

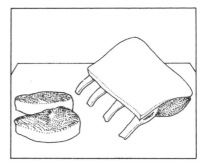

Do not ignore expensive cuts

six on the same income would force you to buy cheaper cuts. So don't imagine you are always under-privileged, organise your shopping and bask a little in the joys of a small household.

HOW LONG WILL IT KEEP?

Extra long keepers

Canned fish in oil and canned meats (not ham, see left)	5 years
Sugar, cubed, granulated and caster sugar	5 years
Canned meat and vegetable meals	2 years
Canned pasta foods in sauce	2 years
Canned soups	2 years
Canned sponge puddings	2 years
Canned vegetables	2 years

Long keepers (1 year)

Blancmange powder, canned fish in tomato sauce, canned fruit, canned juices, canned milk, canned milk puddings, cocoa, cornflour, custard powder, dehydrated foods, drinking chocolate, icing sugar, instant coffee, instant desserts, jams, marmalades, malted milk, oils, packet soups, pasta, rice, sugar, syrup, treacle

Other foods

Baking powder, bicarbonate of soda	2–3 months
Biscuits (according to variety)	3–11 months
Cake mixes	6 months
Carbonated drinks in cans	6–12 months
Canned ham (over 900 g/2 lb)	6 months (keep refrigerated)
Condensed milk	4–6 months
Dried fruit	2–3 months
Dried yeast	up to 6 months
Evaporated milk	6–8 months
Flour	up to 6 months
Herbs, spices, seasonings	up to 6 months
Instant low-fat/skimmed milk powder	2–3 months
Instant potato	9 months
Jellies, gelatine	up to 12 months
Nuts, coconut	up to 1 month
Pastry mixes	6 months
Pulses	6–12 months
Tea, loose coffee	up to 1 month

Storage of Fresh Foods

A well-stocked refrigerator will put variety in your cooking. When cooking for one or two, buy lots of different foods in small quantities— that way there will be no boring days of eating up leftovers. Most foods will keep between three days and a week if bought really fresh and stored properly.

Perishable foods such as meat, fish, dairy produce, salads and leafy green vegetables are best kept in the refrigerator. The

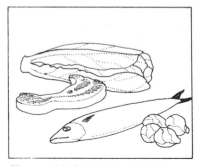

Keep perishable food in the fridge

stronger greens will survive quite well in a cool larder if there is no space in the fridge, along with root vegetables and fruits. For 'larder' storage, choose somewhere where the temperature will not rise above 10°C (50°F), and put them in a well ventilated box or basket.

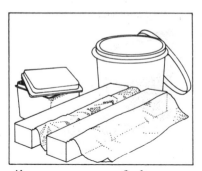

Always cover or wrap foods

Cover or wrap all foods before you put them in the refrigerator, and allow cooked foods to cool first. Warm or uncovered foods cause the frozen food compartment to become frosted up, which will prevent the refrigerator operating efficiently.

Keep raw meat, bacon, poultry and fish in the coldest part of the refrigerator which, if you have a frozen food compartment, will be directly under that. If you have a 'larder fridge' with no frozen food compartment, check the manufacturer's booklet for the coldest area. Keep cooked meats

and made-up dishes in the middle shelves and vegetables and salads at the bottom—in the special box if there is one. The refrigerator door is less cold than the main body of the cabinet and there is usually specially designed storage there for milk bottles, butter and eggs.

Most foods, especially cheese and cooked meats, will taste better if removed from the refrigerator about 30 minutes before serving. This takes the chill off and allows the flavour to come through.

If you spill anything in the refrigerator, wipe it up immediately before it has time to solidify. Remember this is supposed to be a hygienic storage area—stale spilled food is a perfect breeding ground for bacteria. And keep a weather eye out for oddments tucked away in corners and see that they are either eaten quickly or thrown out if necessary.

Defrost the fridge regularly unless it does this automatically— it works more efficiently when frost free. Clean it with a weak

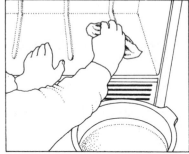

Clean the fridge regularly

solution of bicarbonate of soda in warm water, using a clean cloth. Ordinary soap or detergent tend to leave a penetrating smell which may be absorbed by the stored foods.

REFRIGERATOR STORAGE

Food	How to Store	Number of days
Cheese		
Cream, curd or	Original pack, polythene, cling film or foil	7–14
cottage cheese	Covered container, polythene or foil	2–3
Eggs		
Fresh in shell	Small end down	14
Hard-boiled in shell	Uncovered	up to 7
Whites	Covered container	3–4
Yolks	Covered with water if whole	2–3
Fats	Original wrapper, in door compartments	14–28
Fish		
Cooked	Covered loosely in polythene or foil. Or place in covered container	2
Raw	Covered loosely in polythene or foil	1–2
Fruit and vegetables		
Hard and stone		
fruits	Lightly wrapped or in the crisper	3–7
Salad vegetables	Clean and drain, store in crisper or lightly wrapped in polythene or in a plastic container	4–6
Soft fruits	Clean and refrigerate in a covered container	1–3
Greens	Prepare ready for use. Wrap lightly or place in the crisper	3–7
Milk		
Fresh milk	In bottle or covered container	3–4
Milk puddings, custards, etc.	In covered dishes	2
Cultured milk	In original container	7
Yeast, fresh	In loosely tied polythene bag	up to 28
Cooked meats		
Casseroles with bacon	Wrap in foil or polythene or leave in the covered dish they were cooked in or any other covered container	2
Casseroles without bacon		3
Joints		2
Ham		2–3
Meat pies		1
Pâté		2
Sliced meat with gravy		2–3
Sliced meat without gravy		2–4
Stock		4
Meat		
Uncooked		
Bacon joints: smoked and unsmoked	Wipe surface with clean damp cloth. Cover lightly with polythene or foil Refrigerate straightaway	7
vacuum packed		10
Bacon rashers, chops and steaks:	Wrap tightly in foil or cling film	
smoked and unsmoked		10
vacuum packed		7
Beef		3–5
Mince		1–2
Offal		1–2
Pork		2–4
Sausages		3
Poultry		
Whole fresh poultry	Draw, wash, dry and wrap in polythene or foil. Remove wrappings from ready-to-cook birds	2–3
Cooked poultry	Remove stuffing. Wrap or cover with polythene or foil. Refrigerate straightaway	2–3

Using the Freezer

Freezers are not just for large families needing an endless supply of ice cream and hamburgers. Nor are they only for country dwellers who live miles from the shops. Single people and couples will also find that a freezer, once bought, becomes an integral and necessary part of their way of life.

A freezer is primarily a convenient and healthy method of food storage. If the food is fresh when it goes into the freezer, it will be fresh when it comes out — unlike in a refrigerator where the chill is only sufficient to slow down deterioration, not to stop it.

HEALTH

Food values change very little while food is stored in the freezer, in sharp contrast to other methods of preservation such as bottling and canning, which rely on heat to destroy the spoilage organisms. With these methods, the heat also destroys a high proportion of the food value, especially vitamins. In some cases food which is frozen while at the peak of freshness will have a higher food value than that which may have stood in the village shop for a day or two, and then in your vegetable rack for a day or two more before it finally reaches your plate.

CONVENIENCE

If the nutritional value of frozen food gives you some satisfaction when you happen to think about it, the convenience factor will quite simply change your life. With a freezer in the home you are no longer dependent on daily or even weekly shopping, and you can even regulate your cooking to fit in more conveniently with other demands on your time. Meat, vegetables, fruit, snacks, bread — they and a whole lot more foods can all be frozen, cutting down on the bulk of your regular shopping.

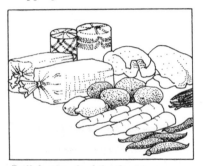

Bulk buying food for freezing

If you own a freezer you can shop monthly where you used to shop weekly. For many seasonal foods such as fruit and vegetables it can even become a once a year event, when you pick, freeze and store enough fresh produce to last you through till next year. Of course there are foods which do not freeze well, and you will want to vary your diet with fresh foods. But the peace of mind that comes from knowing there is always something available to eat is precious to freezer owners.

If all this shopping sounds expensive, remember that buying in bulk is usually less expensive than buying in small quantities. You have to balance these economies against the actual cost of running the freezer — electricity, packaging materials and so on — but in the long run your freezer should not actually cost you money if you run it carefully. What it will do is to improve your standard of living by adding to the variety of foods that are easily accessible to you.

As well as shopping, the freezer can make your cooking more convenient. If when you are

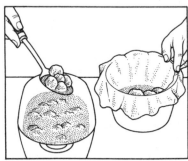

Divide and separate meat to freeze

cooking a casserole you prepare enough for two meals and freeze half, this will save time on another day when you may have less time or energy. You could also actually choose to cook when you otherwise would not need to. If you enjoy cooking you might like to while away a wet Sunday afternoon cooking for the freezer — then on working days reheating is the only work required.

At first thought this may seem the way to repetitive eating, but in practice it usually turns out to be the opposite. In a small household it is all too easy to get into the habit of existing on a limited diet of quickly cooked foods—single chops, single chicken joints, sausages. The freezer will encourage you to ring the changes with more complicated dishes. It will also save waste, as leftovers can be stored properly for use another day.

BULK BUYING

One of the prime advantages of freezer ownership is the facility it gives you for bulk buying. Whether you snap up a cheap offer at the local butcher, or pick your own raspberries in July to enjoy in December, you will appreciate this extension to your normal shopping patterns. But be disciplined. Be sure you want what you are buying and will use it up within a reasonable time. Otherwise the storage will be costing you more than you can possibly save on the purchase price of fresh food.

Watch particularly that you are buying the quality of food that you would normally want—buying inferior goods is no saving. If possible, and particularly if you do not know the supplier, taste a small sample first. This may not be possible with meat, so you are probably best to stick to a supplier you know and trust. But it is often possible for fruit and vegetables; buy enough for one meal first, then go back for more if the quality is good.

Remember that although frozen foods stay healthy almost indefinitely, the eating quality does start to deteriorate with long storage. This is because no packaging is completely vapour-proof and the foods do begin gradually to dry out. This may affect only the surface at first but will eventually penetrate right through the food. Water content

makes up quite a large part of many foods and if this is allowed to evaporate the foods may become tough, chewy, stringy or simply less tasty.

For prepared foods that are easily replaced, plan no more than about 3 months storage. This is particularly important for commercially-packed foods, where you are going to open and reseal the pack; resealing is never as airtight as the original seal. When you are cooking for the freezer at home, it is a matter of pride. You will be less than pleased if a home-made steak and kidney pie is allowed to dry out until it tastes no better than one you could have bought at the corner shop.

Meat is less vulnerable. You can buy it from a freezer centre or have it freshly frozen (ask the butcher to blast freeze it for you if buying fresh meat). Most meats will remain in good condition for a comfortable six months. This period will probably see you through several seasonal price rises, so watch the prices and buy carefully. The exceptions are offal, bacon and minced meats. Offal is best kept for no more than three months, and mince deteriorates quickly because of the large number of cut surfaces exposed to the air. Bacon with other cured and smoked meats, goes rancid and is best eaten within one or two months.

Fresh, seasonal fruit and vegetables are different. It is worth buying a year's supply so long as you are sure the quality is good and you pack it well. On the other hand, don't overdo any one food. Even asparagus can become boring if served too often!

Portioning is important when you buy or cook in bulk. Wherever possible, divide large packs into smaller ones, in meal-size portions. Foods will keep much better if a pack is not frequently opened and closed again. And for foods that freeze into a solid block, it is almost impossible to cut off portions when needed.

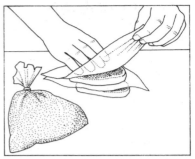

Divide chops with cling film

When buying meat, make sure that it is cut into joints or pieces to suit you. Divide chops with cling film or freezer paper in ones or twos, so that you can separate off what is required as you need it. Pack mince in 225 g (8 oz) or 450 g (1 lb) bags, suitable for one meal or for one cooking session with some left over to freeze away.

When freezing fresh fruit and vegetables, it is possible to achieve a free-flow pack from which you can empty out a little at a time, but difficult. Much better again to buy a supply of small bags and divide up the fruit before freezing.

Take care when freezing fresh food not to put too much into the freezer at once or you will raise the temperature in the cabinet above a safe level. Fast freezing always achieves the best results (small packs help here again), and most freezers have a 'fast freeze' switch which cuts out the thermostat, allowing the temperature to drop well below the normal storage temperature. Most manufacturers recommend that you freeze only 10 per cent of the freezer's total capacity in any 24 hour period. If you do not have a separate fast freeze compartment, which is the case with many small models, try to keep a separate shelf or some other method of preventing the fresh unfrozen foods touching the surfaces of those already in the freezer.

BATCH COOKING

Another joy of the freezer owner is that of cooking two, or several, meals in one go. This rarely takes more time than a single meal of the same dish, and yet saves considerable time when it comes to serving the frozen dish on later occasions. In a small household of one or two people there are also considerable financial economies to be made in savings of fuel. Many people hesitate to switch on the oven to cook a single portion of casserole for two or three hours — but if the oven can be filled with several portions of the same or similar dishes, then it is well worthwhile. For thawing and reheating, a pan on top of the stove or the microwave cooker are often adequate.

There are two main approaches to bulk cooking. The first is the simplest: you cook one big dish such as a stew or pot of soup, divide it into suitable portions and pack them into the freezer. The other is more complicated, and could be thought of as chain cooking. This way you cook a basic item in bulk but turn it into several different dishes for freezing. So a bag full of windfall apples will make stewed apple and also apple sauce, apple pie, blackberry or raspberry and apple pie, apple crumble or apple flans as you wish. For speed, you will appreciate the help of gadgets such as a food processor to slice the apples and rub in the pastry and crumble mixtures quickly, or an electric mixer for beating and creaming cake mixtures.

Batch cooking with minced beef

If you have been tempted by a special offer on minced beef, start by cooking it all together as a basic savoury mixture. You could then, for example, turn one quarter of it into lasagne, another into cottage pie, a third portion into meat loaf, and eke out any left over with beans to make chilli con carne. Whether you make up all these dishes in the first cooking session, or whether you cook and pack the basic mince mixture ready for use later is a matter of choice — either way you save considerable time.

Use chain cooking to add variety to your meals. If you live alone you probably are used to buying single chicken joints to bake or grill. With a freezer installed, try buying two whole chickens. First take off the breasts; these can be frozen flat, for stir frying, or stuffed and rolled ready for frying. Pack them in ones or twos as appropriate. Use the leg and wing joints for casseroles or cook the complete carcasses together, remove the meat and use it for fricassée, curry or chicken and mushroom pies. Stew the bones and giblets for stock and save the livers for pâté or sautés. You will be able to buy whole chickens much more cheaply per 450 g (1 lb) than individual joints, and nothing will be wasted.

The end result of all these ploys is more variety than is otherwise reasonable when cooking for one or two. You also have the fun of cooking when you want to, with reduced work when you don't want it.

PACKAGING

Freezing converts water to ice within the cell structure of the food. If careless packaging allows moisture to be withdrawn from other foods, or from the inside of the freezer, then frosting will appear on the outside of the food. And if it is allowed to continue, moisture will eventually be withdrawn from the food itself, causing dehydration and loss of nutrients.

With meat and poultry this can be particularly noticeable, with exposed areas developing 'freezer burn'. This is the name given when tissues go tough and spongy — so tough and spongy that no amount of clever cooking can put it right. And with any kind of food, strong smells can travel from one faulty package to another, so that a delicate lemon water ice could come out with the flavour of curried beef.

So the basic requirements of freezer packaging are to exclude air from the food, preventing oxidation, and to contain water vapour within the package. The other important thing to remember is labelling; wrapped foods quickly become totally anonymous in the freezer, leading to possibly disastrous, often comic, results when you come to prepare a meal.

There are many different packaging materials on the market, it it is important to use those labelled especially for freezer use. These will be thicker and more completely vapour-proof than those intended for general kitchen use.

Cling film is not really suitable for freezer use as it is not thick enough, and quickly ceases to 'cling' at freezer temperatures. However, it may be useful as an inner wrap for awkwardly shaped foods.

Foil is useful as an inner wrap for awkward shapes such as meat, fish or pies. It can be pressed firmly against the surface of the food to exclude virtually all air. But it punctures easily, so always overwrap with a polythene bag.

Foil dishes These are another favourite standby. They come in all sorts of shapes and sizes — square, round, pie dishes, flan dishes or pudding basins — and some come with a fitting lid. Beware of buying a manufacturer's pack of foil dishes of mixed sizes — there will be lots you will not use. Much better to buy a few

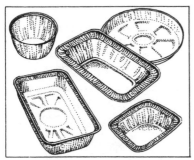

Foil containers for freezing

individual dishes until you find which ones best suit your needs, then buy those in bulk. If thoroughly washed and checked for holes, foil dishes can be reused several times. The lids cannot be reused, however, as they are backed with card which is not washable, so for second use they must be covered with foil and overwrapped with a polythene bag.

Labelling Waterproof labels are vital. Anything else will fall off in the freezer and you will be left not knowing what is what. Equally important is a waterproof pen that will not smudge and become illegible.

Microwave dishes If you intend using your freezer in combination with a microwave cooker, look for microwave-safe plastic dishes. These can be used for storage in the freezer and transferred directly to the microwave for thawing and reheating.

Re-usable plastic boxes Rigid plastic boxes with an airtight snap-on lid are expensive but useful for fragile pastries and cakes, and they last for years. If you save manufacturer's plastic boxes you may be able to avoid the expense of buying these. Ice cream cartons are ideal, and last well. Margarine boxes and tubs, yogurt pots and cottage cheese tubs, etc., are all useful, but they do become brittle in the freezer so cannot be re-used indefinitely.

Polythene bags Many people manage almost entirely with polythene bags. Always choose heavy duty bags, and they can be washed, dried and reused several times. But do check that they have not been punctured during use. Buy a selection of different sizes to start with and you will soon learn which you find most useful.

Fasten bags with paper or plastic covered twist ties, excluding as much air as possible from the package.

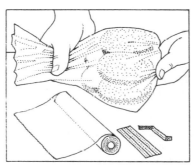

Exclude air from bag before tying

Boilable bags are more expensive but are especially useful for microwave owners. They must be sealed with the special plastic ties provided if you are going to use them in the microwave (metal ties will cause arcing). With these bags the food can be thawed and reheated without removing it from the bag.

Waxed freezer paper is primarily useful for portioning. You can use it to interleave individual chops or fillets of fish, or individual portions of cake or pâté, so that you can pack a large quantity in one bag or box, removing individual portions as required.

Packing for one or two Finally, if you are alone or a couple, always pack for one or two unless you are cooking for a specific special occasion. You can always open 2 packs if you have visitors.

Leftovers

When cooking for one or two, the tendency is to restrict the choice of dishes to those for which you can buy exactly the right quantity of ingredients. With a little imagination and careful storage, you can use the same ingredients for several meals without any danger of monotony.

MEAT

So many delicious dishes can be made with a small amount of leftover roast meat or poultry that it is worth cooking a joint or whole chicken just for one or two.

Bacon Is perfect reheated. A small bacon joint, boiled or baked for one meal, leaves ideal amounts of meat to put with chicken in a pie, to make a sauce for tagliatelle with cream and herbs or to chop for an omelette. Thickly sliced boiled bacon is also good lightly fried and served with a fruit glaze.

Beef The best beef for leftovers is that which has been roasted rare, leaving the cold meat pink and juicy. Take it off the bone for storage, removing any excess fat as you work. Fat is never tasty reheated, however much you like it on the outside of a roast joint. When mincing cooked beef, use the coarsest blade you can, or preferably chop the meat finely

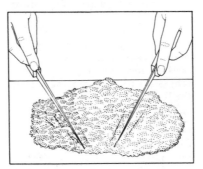

Chopping meat finely with knives

with knives; finely minced cooked beef is inclined to turn to a paste.

When it comes to using up cooked beef, few people will say no to a simple plate of cold sliced meat. But if you are bored with that, or there are only messy ends left, try a real bubble and squeak. You can use leftover cabbage, but it is best made with freshly cooked cabbage that is still crisp. Fry the roughly chopped cooked cabbage lightly in butter, add small slices of beef and heat through with some of the leftover gravy

and some seasonings like Worcestershire sauce and perhaps sliced gherkins or pickled onions. It will squeak and bubble as it cooks, and will taste delicious.

Use leftovers as a stuffing

Alternatively use the beef to stuff green peppers or giant tomatoes, onions or baked potatoes. Mixed with a spicy tomato sauce and rice, or the middle of the potato, it is almost worth cooking beef especially to have some left over.

Chicken The best chicken meat for reheated dishes comes from a boiled chicken as it remains moister than a roast bird, but cold chicken is always acceptable in a new dish. A chicken pie, with a little ham or bacon and a puff pastry top gives no hint that it is leftover meat. A savoury chicken pancake, the filling made with a good béchamel sauce and perhaps a few mushrooms and herbs to add flavour to a small amount of meat makes a perfect evening snack. Chicken does not mince well, the flesh is too fine and turns paste-

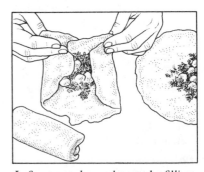

Leftovers make good pancake fillings

like in a mincer, so always chop or shred the meat for reheating.

Never throw away the carcass and giblets from a chicken. They make excellent stock or soup, especially if there is a little meat left on the bones. Add some finely chopped vegetables or rice to bulk out the soup.

Lamb Take care not to overcook lamb the first time round. As long as it is young and tender, lamb is best served when still lightly pink in the centre, and cooking it like this will mean that it does not become hard and chewy when reheated. If you are not planning to eat it straightaway, the leftover meat will keep best if removed from the bone. Cut it off the bone in the largest chunks possible, wrap tightly in foil and keep in the refrigerator for up to four days. Do not mince, slice or cube it until you are ready to use it; the more cut surfaces there are exposed to the air, the more quickly it will go off.

For mincing, the leaner leg is best, although the shoulder meat is sometimes sweeter and many people prefer it. Cut most of the fat off shoulder meat before mincing or slicing for reheating. Shepherd's pie is the traditional English way of using up roast lamb, and there are many exciting dishes from Greece and the Eastern end of the Mediterranean based on lamb. Moussaka is the classic, while stuffed aubergines are a delicious variation. In the North African tradition, you could try meatballs seasoned with garlic and coriander—make tiny ones to serve as an unusual snack with drinks. Apart from mint, the traditional herbs to put with lamb are garlic, rosemary and thyme, while ground coriander and a good garam masala powder will spice it appropriately.

Pork Leftover pork is more limited in use, as it should always be thoroughly cooked in the first place and reheating is inclined to harden it. It is best combined with other meats in a meat loaf or meatballs, or layered up with cabbage leaves and tomato sauce to make a Dutch-style stuffed cabbage dish.

VEGETABLES

Large whole vegetables that cannot be bought divided sometimes pose problems in a small household, but there are many ways of getting round them.

Aubergine Is good sliced and grilled or fried, in a ratatouille or a moussaka. A half aubergine also forms the base for a main meal if stuffed with a good meaty filling.

Avocado Will go black if cut and left, so if you eat one half with vinaigrette, you must do something with the other half straightaway to keep it in good condition. Puréed, seasoned with a little lemon juice and covered with 0.5 cm ($\frac{1}{4}$ inch) of oil it will keep in the refrigerator for a few days. Mix the purée with cream cheese or soured cream and seasonings for a dip to serve with snacks and drinks, or a Mexican-style meal.

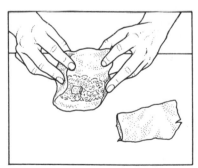

Use cabbage leaves for wrapping

Cabbage When you have eaten half a Savoy-type cabbage as a vegetable, use the other half layered up with sausagemeat and tomato sauce in a stuffed cabbage dish, or to make cabbage rolls (*dolmas*). White cabbage keeps extremely well in a cool place, and makes excellent coleslaw.

Celery A whole head of celery can go on for ever for one person, so just use the inside stalks for salad. The outer stalks are good braised, or for soup or chopped in a stew. Chop the leaves for garnishes.

Lettuce The crisp varieties keep best, even if they do look bigger than the traditional roundhead soft-leaved variety. Iceberg lettuces keep particularly well— you can just slice off what is needed for any meal and pop the rest back in the refrigerator.

Marrow A whole marrow may look a giant if you face it on your own, but you can use it in many different ways. Peel and roast some of it with a joint for a really tasty, seasonal vegetable, then stuff the rest with minced leftovers later in the week. Cover the cut surface tightly with cling film and it will keep for several days. For a change, blanch it and use in a salad. If you are given a giant marrow, turn it into chutney.

Peppers Green, red and yellow peppers are excellent cooked, in casseroles, and in salads. Half a pepper or some leftover chopped pepper will keep in the refrigerator for several days.

Pumpkin May not be something you want to eat every day, but it is fun to have once in a season. You can use it as a vegetable, roasted with the joint or fried in butter. It can also be used to make a sweet pie, puréed and spiced.

Basic Recipes

This immensely useful chapter is packed with basic recipes to help you with the dishes in the front section of the book, from sauces and dressings through to pastries, pasta and pizza.

Dressings and Sauces

BASIC VINAIGRETTE

Makes 135 ml (9 tbsp)

90 ml (6 tbsp) olive oil

45 ml (3 tbsp) wine vinegar or lemon juice

2.5 ml ($\frac{1}{2}$ tsp) caster sugar

2.5 ml ($\frac{1}{2}$ tsp) wholegrain, Dijon or French mustard

salt and freshly ground pepper

1 Place all the ingredients in a bowl or screw-topped jar and whisk or shake together.

2 Before use, whisk or shake dressing again, as the oil separates out on standing. Taste and adjust seasoning.

Note
If a recipe calls for 150 ml ($\frac{1}{4}$ pint) of dressing, add an extra 15 ml (1 tbsp) oil.

─────── VARIATIONS ───────

Try also **tarragon vinegar** in dressings for tomatoes or potatoes; **thyme vinegar** with eggs or mushrooms; **cider vinegar** with fruits.
Sunflower oil alone or half and half with **olive oil** makes a lighter dressing.
Walnut or **sesame oil** adds interest to strongly-flavoured ingredients.

MAYONNAISE

Makes about 150 ml ($\frac{1}{4}$ pint)

1 egg yolk

2.5 ml ($\frac{1}{2}$ tsp) mustard powder

salt and freshly ground white pepper

150 ml ($\frac{1}{4}$ pint) olive or vegetable oil

15 ml (1 tbsp) white wine vinegar or lemon juice

1 Put the egg yolk into a small bowl. Beat in the mustard powder and salt and pepper.

2 Add 30 ml (2 tbsp) oil, drop by drop, beating vigorously after adding. Beat in 5 ml (1 tsp) of the vinegar or lemon juice.

3 Gradually beat in the remaining oil until the mixture becomes very thick. Add the remaining vinegar to taste. Store in a screw-topped jar for up to 1 week in the refrigerator.

HOLLANDAISE SAUCE

Makes about 150 ml ($\frac{1}{4}$ pint)

2.5 ml ($\frac{1}{2}$ tsp) lemon juice

2.5 ml ($\frac{1}{2}$ tsp) white wine vinegar

2 peppercorns

1 small bay leaf

2 egg yolks

salt and freshly ground pepper

100 g (4 oz) unsalted butter, softened

1 Put the lemon juice, vinegar, peppercorns and bay leaf into a small saucepan with 10 ml (2 tsp) water. Boil until the liquid is reduced by half. Cool.

2 Put the egg yolks into a small bowl, add a pinch of salt and 15 g ($\frac{1}{2}$ oz) of the butter and beat well. Strain in the vinegar and mix.

3 Put the bowl into a saucepan of boiling water and turn off the heat. Beat the mixture until it begins to thicken, then beat in the remaining butter in small pieces. Once all the butter has been absorbed by the sauce, taste and season with salt and pepper. Serve warm with fish, egg, chicken and vegetable dishes. Do not reheat or the mixture will curdle.

BÉARNAISE SAUCE

Makes about 150 ml ($\frac{1}{4}$ pint)

45 ml (3 tbsp) white wine vinegar

6 black peppercorns

1 small bay leaf

1 blade mace

1 slice onion

2 tarragon leaves

2 egg yolks

salt and freshly ground pepper

100 g (4 oz) unsalted butter, softened

10 ml (2 tsp) meat glaze, or jelly at the base of beef dripping (optional)

5 ml (1 tsp) mixed chopped tarragon, parsley and chervil

5 ml (1 tsp) snipped fresh chives

1 Put the vinegar, peppercorns, bay leaf, mace, onion and tarragon leaves into a small saucepan. Boil until the vinegar has reduced to 15 ml (1 tbsp). Cool.

2 Put the egg yolks into a small bowl with 15 g ($\frac{1}{2}$ oz) of the butter and a pinch of salt. Cream together, strain in the vinegar and beat well.

3 Put the bowl into a saucepan of boiling water and turn off the heat. Beat the mixture until it begins to thicken. Beat in the remaining butter in small pieces and then the meat glaze, if using. Season to taste and stir in the herbs. Serve warm with grilled meats. Do not reheat or the mixture will curdle.

BASIC WHITE (POURING) SAUCE

Makes 300 ml ($\frac{1}{2}$ pint)

15 g ($\frac{1}{2}$ oz) butter

15 g ($\frac{1}{2}$ oz) plain flour

300 ml ($\frac{1}{2}$ pint) milk

salt and freshly ground pepper

1 Melt the butter in a saucepan. Add the flour and cook over low heat, stirring with a wooden spoon, for 2 minutes. Do not allow the mixture (roux) to brown.

2 Remove the pan from the heat and gradually blend in the milk, stirring after each addition to prevent lumps forming. Bring to the boil slowly and continue to cook, stirring all the time, until the sauce comes to the boil and thickens.

3 Once thickened, simmer the sauce very gently for a further 2–3 minutes. Season with salt and freshly ground pepper.

——————— VARIATIONS ———————

COATING SAUCE
Follow the recipe for Pouring Sauce (above), but increase butter and flour to 25 g (1 oz) each.

CHEESE SAUCE
Follow the recipe for Pouring Sauce or Coating Sauce (above). Before seasoning, stir in **50 g (2 oz) grated Cheddar cheese** and **2.5 ml ($\frac{1}{2}$ tsp) mustard**.

PARSLEY SAUCE
Follow the recipe for Pouring Sauce or Coating Sauce. Before seasoning, add **15–30 ml (1–2 tbsp) chopped fresh parsley**. Season well.

SIMPLE TOMATO SAUCE

Makes about 150 ml ($\frac{1}{4}$ pint)

450 g (1 lb) tomatoes, skinned and roughly chopped, or 397 g (14 oz) can tomatoes, with their juice

1 small onion, skinned and roughly chopped

1 garlic clove, skinned and chopped

1 celery stick, sliced

1 bay leaf

sprig of parsley

2.5 ml ($\frac{1}{2}$ tsp) caster sugar

salt and freshly ground pepper

1 Place all the ingredients in a saucepan and bring to the boil. Simmer, uncovered, for 30 minutes until thickened . Stir occasionally to prevent sticking to the bottom of the pan.

2 Remove the bay leaf and purée the mixture in an electric blender or food processor until smooth, or push through a sieve using a wooden spoon. Reheat, then taste and adjust seasoning. Serve hot or leave to cool and store in a covered bowl in the refrigerator for up to 5 days. Or freeze for up to 3 months.

NEAPOLITAN TOMATO SAUCE

Makes about 450 ml ($\frac{3}{4}$ pint)

350 g (12 oz) tomatoes, skinned and roughly chopped, or a 226 g (8 oz) can tomatoes, with their juice

1 garlic clove, skinned and crushed

30 ml (2 tbsp) olive oil

1 sprig of fresh oregano, marjoram, basil or parsley, or 1.25 ml ($\frac{1}{4}$ tsp) dried

1.25 ml ($\frac{1}{4}$ tsp) sugar

salt and freshly ground pepper

1 Place all the ingredients in a saucepan and bring to the boil.

2 Lower the heat and simmer, uncovered, for about 10 minutes until the oil has separated from the tomatoes. Stir frequently.

3 Taste and adjust seasoning. Serve hot, or leave to cool and store in a covered bowl in the refrigerator for up to 4 days. Or freeze for up to 3 months.

PASTRIES AND BREADS

Pastries are versatile and can be used for savoury or sweet dishes. Breads can accompany soups or can form a meal in their own right when sandwiched with tasty ingredients.

SHORTCRUST PASTRY

For shortcrust pastry, use half the quantity of fat to flour. Therefore for a recipe using quantities of shortcrust pastry other than 225 g (8 oz), simply use half the quantity of fat to flour weight specified.

| 225 g (8 oz) plain flour |
| pinch of salt |
| 50 g (2 oz) butter or margarine |
| 50 g (2 oz) lard |

1 Sift the flour and salt in to a bowl. Cut the butter or margarine and lard into small pieces and add to the flour.

2 Lightly rub in the butter or margarine and the lard with your fingertips until the mixture resembles fine breadcrumbs.

3 Add 30–45 ml (2–3 tbsp) chilled water evenly over the surface and stir in until the mixture begins to stick together in large lumps.

4 With one hand, collect the mixture together to form a ball. Knead lightly for a few seconds to give a firm, smooth dough. Do not over-handle.

5 The pastry can be used straightaway, but it is better if allowed to 'rest' for about 30 minutes wrapped in foil in the refrigerator.

6 When the pastry is required, sprinkle a very little flour on the working surface and on the rolling pin, not on the pastry, and roll out the dough evenly in one direction only, turning occasionally. Roll out to a thickness of about 3 mm ($\frac{1}{8}$ inch). Do not pull or stretch the pastry. To cook, the usual oven temperature for shortcrust pastry is 200–220°C (400–425°F) mark 6–7.

Freezing: Both baked and unbaked shortcrust pastry and wholemeal pastry freeze well, although care should be taken when handling frozen baked pastry as it is very fragile. Wrap the pastry tightly in freezer film and place in a polythene bag. Freeze for up to 3 months. Thaw unbaked dough at room temperature before unwrapping, but rolled-out pastry cases may be cooked from frozen.

A 368 g (13 oz) packet of frozen shortcrust pastry is equivalent to a 225 g (8 oz) flour weight.

WHOLEMEAL PASTRY

For wholemeal pastry the proportion of flour to fat is two to one. Therefore, for a recipe requiring 250 g (8 oz) pastry, make up the pastry using 250 g (8 oz) flour and 125 g (4 oz) fat.

When a recipe requires 175 g (6 oz) pastry, this refers to the weight of flour.

| 175 g (6 oz) plain wholemeal flour |
| pinch of salt |
| 75 g (3 oz) margarine or butter |

1 Mix the flour and salt together in a bowl and add the margarine in small pieces. Using both hands, rub the margarine into the flour between finger and thumb tips until there are no lumps of margarine left and the mixture resembles fine breadcrumbs.

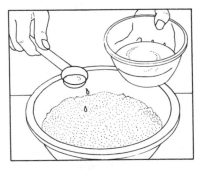

2 Add 30 ml (2 tbsp) water all at once, sprinkling it evenly over the surface.

3 Stir in the water with a round-bladed knife until the mixture begins to stick together in large lumps.

4 With one hand, collect the mixture together and knead lightly for a few seconds, to give a firm smooth dough. The pastry can be used straightaway, but is better allowed to 'rest' for 15 minutes. It can also be wrapped in polythene and kept in the refrigerator for 1–2 days.

5 When the pastry is required, sprinkle a very little flour on the working surface and on the rolling pin, not on the pastry, and roll out the dough evenly in one direction only, turning occasionally. The usual thickness is about 3 mm ($\frac{1}{8}$ inch). Do not pull or stretch the dough. Use as required. The usual oven temperature for wholemeal pastry is 200–220°C (400–425°F) mark 6–7.

QUICK FLAKY PASTRY

100 g (4 oz) block margarine

175 g (6 oz) plain flour

pinch of salt

about 30 ml (2 tbsp) chilled water

1 Place the margarine in the freezer and freeze for at least 3 hours until solid.

2 Put the flour and salt in a bowl and coarsely grate in the frozen margarine.

3 Add enough chilled water to bind the mixture together to form a dough.

4 Wrap the dough in foil or cling film and leave to 'rest' in the refrigerator for about 30 minutes. Roll out as for shortcrust pastry.

Freezing and storing: Wrap and freeze as for shortcrust pastry. This pastry does not keep well in the refrigerator.

QUICK WHOLEMEAL ROLLS

Makes 12

15 g ($\frac{1}{2}$ oz) fresh yeast or $7\frac{1}{2}$ g ($\frac{1}{4}$ oz) dried

10 ml (2 tsp) sugar

225 g (8 oz) strong white flour

225 g (8 oz) strong wholemeal flour

10 ml (2 tsp) salt

15 g ($\frac{1}{2}$ oz) lard

cracked wheat, for the topping (optional)

1 Blend the yeast with 5 ml (1 tsp) sugar and 300 ml ($\frac{1}{2}$ pint) tepid water and leave in a warm place to froth.

2 Mix both flours together in a bowl with the salt and the remaining 5 ml (1 tsp) sugar. Rub in the fat.

3 Add the yeast mixture and mix to a soft dough. Turn on to a lightly floured surface and knead for about 2 minutes until smooth.

4 Divide the dough into 12 equal pieces and roll into rounds. Place on a greased baking sheet, brush with water and sprinkle the tops with cracked wheat.

5 Cover the rolls with a clean, damp tea towel and leave to rise in a warm place for about 1 hour or until doubled in size.

6 Bake the rolls in the oven at 230°C (450°F) mark 8 for 15–20 minutes or until golden brown. Cool on a wire rack.

PASTA

Fresh pasta is the all-time favourite in its simplicity and versatility. Economical to make, it can be varied by the addition of spinach or tomato to colour it and can be cooked in a variety of sauces. It will keep for 2–3 days if covered and stored in the refrigerator.

PASTA QUANTITIES

When calculating quantities of fresh or dried pasta per person, remember that they are exactly the same: fresh pasta is lighter in weight than dried, but it almost trebles in weight when cooked.

Italians always eat pasta as a course on its own, after the anti-pasto and before the main course. If you are serving pasta as a starter before a substantial main course dish, then you will need 50–75 g (2–3 oz) pasta per person. If you are serving pasta as a main course dish for an informal meal, then increase the quantity to 100–175 g (4–6 oz) per person.

BASIC EGG PASTA

Makes about 350 g (12 oz) dough

about 200 g (7 oz) strong plain flour or semolina flour

2 eggs, beaten

pinch of salt

15 ml (1 tbsp) olive oil

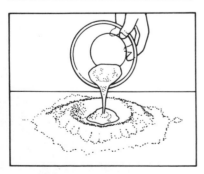

1 Sift the flour into a mound on a clean work surface. With your fist, make a well in the centre and add the eggs, salt and oil.

2 Using your fingertips, gradually stir in the flour from the sides of the well. Continue until the dough comes together.

3 Then, using both hands, knead the dough for about 10 minutes until smooth and not sticky.

4 Wrap the dough in cling film and leave to rest in a cool place for 30 minutes.

5 Roll out the pasta on a floured work surface to a large rectangle which is nearly paper thin.

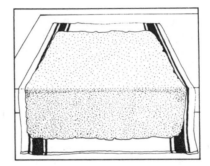

6 If you are making cut pasta such as tagliatelle, fettuccine or lasagne, the dough must be allowed to dry. Place the dough on a clean tea towel, allowing one third to hang over the edge of a table or work surface. Turn every 10 minutes.

7 The pasta is ready to cut after about 30 minutes, when it is dry to the touch and begins to look leathery.

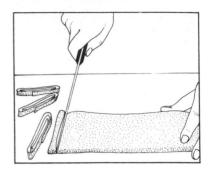

8 To make tagliatelle: fold the dough over into a roll about 8 cm (3 inches) wide. With a sharp knife, cut into 1 cm ($\frac{1}{2}$ inch) wide strips. Try to cut the strips all the same width. After cutting, unfold and leave to dry for a minimum of 10 minutes.

9 To make fettuccine: proceed as for tagliatelle, but cut into 0.5 cm ($\frac{1}{4}$ inch) wide strips.

10 To make lasagne: cut into 10 × 15 cm (4 × 6 inch) rectangles.

—— VARIATION ——

Wash, drain and discard coarse stalks from **225 g (8 oz) fresh spinach**. Cook the leaves in a saucepan, with no additional water until tender, about 5 minutes. Drain and cool, then squeeze out all excess moisture with your hands. Chop finely. Increase the **flour** to **225 g (8 oz)** and add the spinach with the eggs.

WHOLEMEAL PASTA

Makes about 350 g (12 oz)

175 g (6 oz) plain wholemeal flour

1 egg

1 egg white

30 ml (2 tbsp) olive oil

5 ml (1 tsp) salt

1 Place the flour in a large bowl. Make a well in the centre and add the egg, egg white, oil, salt and 15 ml (1 tbsp) water. Mix together to form a soft dough.

2 Knead the dough for 10 minutes on a lightly floured surface until smooth and elastic. Re-flour the surface and roll out the dough to form a large paper-thin rectangle of pasta.

3 Lay the pasta on a clean dry cloth. Let one third of the pasta sheet hang over the side of the table and turn it every 10 minutes. This will help to dry the pasta more quickly.

4 The drying process takes about 30 minutes and the pasta is ready to cut when it is dry and looks leathery.

5 To make noodles, roll the pasta up loosely into a roll about 7.5 cm (3 inches) wide.

6 Cut the roll into 0.5 cm ($\frac{1}{4}$ inch) slices, unroll and leave for 10 minutes.

7 To serve, cook in boiling salted water for about 8 minutes until just tender.

8 To make lasagne, cut the pasta dough into the desired size of rectangles. Leave on a floured tea towel for 10 minutes before using.

Serving Suggestion
Toss hot drained noodles in a little butter, then sprinkle with black pepper, herbs, ham and grated cheese.

TO COOK PASTA

1.7 litres (3 pints) water
15 ml (1 tbsp) salt
15 ml (1 tbsp) vegetable oil

1 In a very large saucepan, bring the water to the boil. Add the salt and swirl in the oil.

2 When the water is boiling very rapidly, drop in the pasta all at once. (This quantity of water is sufficient to cook 100–225 g (4–8 oz) fresh or dried pasta—do not attempt to cook more than this at one time or the pasta will stick.) Turn up the heat and quickly return the water to the boil. Calculate the cooking time from this moment, according to the following cooking times:

Unfilled pasta
Fresh wholemeal: 8–10 minutes
Fresh white flour pasta: 2–3 minutes
Dried wholemeal pasta: 12–15 minutes
Dried white flour pasta: 8–12 minutes
Filled pasta
Fresh white flour: 8–10 minutes
Fresh wholemeal: 12–15 minutes
Dried white flour: 15–20 minutes
Dried wholemeal: 18–22 minutes

3 Drain the pasta in a colander immediately the cooking time is up. Allow time for all the water to drain thoroughly off the pasta, then pile into a warmed serving dish and toss with sauce, etc., according to individual recipes.

BOLOGNESE SAUCE

Makes enough to dress 2 servings of pasta

15 ml (1 tbsp) olive oil
25 g (1 oz) butter
2 rashers of pancetta or smoked streaky bacon, rinded and finely chopped
1 small onion, skinned and finely chopped
175 g (6 oz) minced beef
1 garlic clove, skinned and finely chopped
1 small celery stick, finely chopped
1 small carrot, peeled and finely chopped
1 bay leaf
15 ml (1 tbsp) tomato purée
75 ml (5 tbsp) dry white wine
75 ml (5 tbsp) beef stock
salt and freshly ground pepper

1 Heat the oil and butter in a small saucepan and fry the pancetta or bacon and chopped onion for 2–3 minutes until soft.

2 Add the minced beef and cook for a further 5 minutes, stirring constantly to break up any lumps, until it is lightly browned.

3 Add the garlic, celery, carrot and bay leaf and cook, stirring, for a further 2 minutes.

4 Stir in the tomato purée, wine, stock and seasoning. Bring to the boil, then lower the heat, cover and simmer for 1–1$\frac{1}{2}$ hours, stirring occasionally. Discard the bay leaf.

5 Taste and adjust seasoning before serving hot, with freshly cooked pasta.

Note
Cover and store in the refrigerator for up to 3 days or freeze for up to 3 months.

PIZZA DOUGHS

Pizza dough, like bread, can be varied according to the flour and liquid used. Easy to make and handy to have in the freezer they can be topped in a variety of ways.

BASIC PIZZA DOUGH

Enough to make two 27.5 cm (11 inch) pizzas, or four 20 cm (8 inch) pizzas

45 ml (3 tbsp) lukewarm milk

20 g ($\frac{3}{4}$ oz) fresh yeast

3.75 ml ($\frac{3}{4}$ tsp) sugar

300 g (11 oz) strong white bread flour

7.5 ml ($1\frac{1}{2}$ tsp) salt

30 ml (2 tbsp) olive oil

1 Put the milk in a warmed jug and crumble in the yeast with your fingers. Add the sugar and stir to dissolve, then stir in 4 tbsp of the flour.

2 Cover the jug with a clean tea towel and leave in a warm place for about 30 minutes or until frothy.

3 Sift the remaining flour and the salt into a warmed large bowl. Mix in the yeast with a fork, then add the oil and enough lukewarm water—about 90 ml (6 tbsp)—to draw the mixture together.

4 Turn the dough out on to a floured surface and knead for 10 minutes until it is smooth and elastic.

5 Put the ball of dough in a large floured bowl, cover with a clean tea towel and leave in a warm place for $1\frac{1}{2}$–2 hours until doubled in bulk.

6 Roll out into the shape required.

Note
Pizza dough freezes extremely well.

WHOLEMEAL PIZZA DOUGH

Serves 1

15 g ($\frac{1}{2}$ oz) fresh yeast or 10 ml (2 tsp) dried and 2.5 ml ($\frac{1}{2}$ tsp) caster sugar

120 ml (8 tbsp) tepid milk

175 g (6 oz) plain wholemeal flour

pinch of salt

40 g ($1\frac{1}{2}$ oz) butter or margarine

1 egg, beaten

1 Blend the fresh yeast into the milk. If using dried yeast, dissolve the sugar in the milk and sprinkle over the yeast. Leave the fresh or dried yeast in a warm place for 15 minutes until frothy.

2 Mix the flour and salt together in a bowl. Rub in the butter, then stir in the yeast mixture and egg.

3 Knead on a floured surface for 10 minutes. Place in the bowl, cover with a tea towel and rise in a warm place for 1 hour until doubled in size.

4 Knead the dough and roll out to a 20.5 cm (8 inch) round. Use as required.

QUICK PIZZA DOUGH

Makes two 27.5 cm (11 inch) pizzas

225 g ($\frac{1}{2}$ lb) self-raising flour

5 ml (1 tsp) salt

50 g (2 oz) butter or margarine

150 ml ($\frac{1}{4}$ pint) milk

1 Sift the flour and salt into a bowl, then rub in the butter until the mixture resembles fine breadcrumbs.

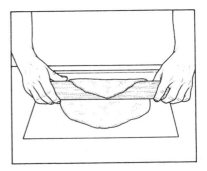

2 Add the milk and mix to a soft dough. Turn out on to a lightly floured work surface and knead until smooth. Cut the dough in half and roll out each piece to a 27.5 cm (11 inch) round.

3 Alternatively, you can use a 284 g (10 oz) packet of white bread mix following the instructions on the packet.

INDEX

Almonds:
  Courgettes and almonds 103
Anchovies:
  Tagliatelle with anchovies 20
Apples:
  Apple gingerbread 124
  Bacon, cheese and apple
    smokies 41
  Chilled apple and avocado
    soup 14
Artichokes:
  Stuffed globe artichoke 23
Asparagus soup 13
Aubergines:
  using leftovers 151
  Chakchouka 100
  Lamb and aubergine curry 52
Avocado:
  using leftovers 151
  Calf's liver with sage and
    avocado 93
  Chilled apple and avocado
    soup 14

Bacon:
  freezing 147
  storing 144, 145
  using leftovers 150
  Bacon, cheese and apple
    smokies 41
  Bacon, lettuce and tomato
    toasted sandwich 42
  Bacon olives 56
  Wilted salad 107
Baked egg with mushrooms 30
Bananas:
  Boozy banana 120
Bean curd 10
Beans, French:
  French beans with water
    chestnuts 103
Béarnaise sauce 153
Beef:
  reheating 150
  using leftovers 150
  Chinese beef with
    mushrooms and oyster
    sauce 55
  Filets de boeuf en croûte 80
  Hot and sour soup 10
  Individual cottage pie 49
  Roquefort rumpburgers 53
Blenders 135
Bolognese sauce 157
Boozy banana 120
Bread:
  French bread pizza 39
  Quick wholemeal rolls 155
Brûlées, tangerine 114
Buck rarebit 38
Bulk buying for the freezer
  147–8
Buttered salmon steaks 75

Cabbage:
  using leftovers 151
Cakes:
  Cut-and-come-again fruit
    cake 123

Rich chocolate cake 127
Calcium, main sources of
  138–9
Calf's liver with sage and
  avocado 93
Californian club sandwich 42
Cans, storing 143
Carbohydrates 136
  Carbohydrate-controlled
    diets 139–40
Carrots:
  Carrot and celeriac
    vinaigrette 24
  Potato, carrot and onion
    casserole 95
Casseroles:
  storing 145
  Potato, carrot and onion
    casserole 95
Cauliflower, souffléed 96
Celeriac:
  Carrot and celeriac
    vinaigrette 24
Celery:
  using leftovers 151
Cereals, storing 142–3
Chakchouka 100
Cheese:
  storing 144, 145
  Bacon, cheese and apple
    smokies 41
  Buck rarebit 38
  Californian club sandwich
    42
  Cheese sauce 153
  Cheesy salami gratin 45
  Croque monsieur 36
  French bread pizza 39
  Roquefort rumpburger 53
  Welsh rarebit 38
Cheesecakes, raspberry 117
Cheese, cream:
  Smoked salmon and cream
    cheese pâté 17
Chicken:
  freezing 147, 148
  using leftovers 150–1
  Californian club sandwich
    42
  Chicken jambalaya 60
  Hot and sour soup 10
  Hot pitta packet 44
  Pan-grilled chicken breasts
    with herbs 63
  Poussins with cream and
    grapes 86
Chinese beef with mushrooms
  and oyster sauce 55
Chocolate:
  Hot chocolate soufflé 113
  Rich chocolate cake 127
Cholesterol 140
  Cholesterol-lowering diets
    140–1
Chowder, ham 13
Cider vinegar (in dressings)
  152
Coffee makers 135
Cookers:
  microwave cookers 131
  multi-cookers 131
  slow cookers 131–2
  table-top ovens 130–1

Cottage pie, individual 49
Courgettes and almonds 103
Crab noodle soup 9
Croque monsieur 36
Curry, lamb and aubergine 52
Cut-and-come-again fruit cake
  123

Deep fat fryers 132
Desserts:
  Boozy banana 120
  Hot chocolate soufflé 113
  Individual plum puddings
    118
  Plum croûte 121
  Raspberry cheesecakes 117
  Sabayon 110
  Sweet soufflé omelette 109
  Tangerine brûlées 114
Diets:
  cholesterol-lowering 140–1
  slimming 139–40
  vegetarian 141
Dishwashers 133
Dressings 152–3
Duckling:
  Peking duck with pancakes
    89

Eggs:
  storing 145
  Baked egg with mushrooms
    30
  Buck rarebit 38
  Egg and spinach croûte 32
  Egg Benedict 29
  Lettuce and mushroom cocotte
    26
  Omelette niçoise 31
  Smoked haddock scramble
    35
  Sweet soufflé omelette 109
Equipment, kitchen 130–5
Escalopes de veau flambé 85

Fats 137
  storing 145
Fettuccine:
  making 156
  Fettuccine in creamy ham
    and mushroom sauce 73
Filets de boeuf en croûte 80
Fish:
  storing 144, 145
  storing canned 143
  Buttered salmon steaks 75
  Lemon and mustard
    mackerel 67
  Marinated kipper fillets 19
  Omelette niçoise 31
  Pizza marinara 71
  Poached trout with fennel 76
  Smoked haddock scramble 35
  Smoked salmon and cream
    cheese pâté 17
  Tagliatelle with anchovies 20
  Tapénade 25
  Whiting in soured cream
    with tomatoes 68
Flour, storing 142–3
Food processors 134–5
Freezers:
  advantages of 146–7

batch cooking for 148
  bulk buying for 147
  choosing 132–3
  packaging of food for 148–9
French beans with water
  chestnuts 103
French bread pizza 39
Fruit see Apples, Bananas etc.
  freezing 147–8
  storing 145
  storing canned 143
Fruit, dried:
  Cut-and-come-again fruit
    cake 123
  Individual plum puddings
    118

Gingerbread apple 124
Glazed spicy sausages 47
Globe artichoke, stuffed 23

Haddock, smoked:
  Smoked haddock scramble
    35
Ham:
  storing 145
  storing canned 143
  Croque monsieur 36
  Ham chowder 13
Hollandaise sauce 152

Iron, main sources of 138

Jam, storing 143
Jambalaya, chicken 60
Japanese salad 106

Kettles, electric 134
Kipper fillets, marinated 19
Knives, kitchen 134

Lamb:
  using leftovers 151
  Hot and sour soup 10
  Lamb and aubergine curry 52
  Lamb noisettes in port and
    redcurrant sauce 82
  Sauté of lamb with courgettes
    and mushrooms 50
Lasagne 156, 157
Leftovers, using up 150–1
Lemons:
  Lemon and mustard
    mackerel 67
  Sabayon 110
Lentils:
  Lentil hot pot 99
  Spicy sausages with lentils
    60
Lettuce 151
  Lettuce and mushroom
    cocotte 26
Liver:
  Calf's liver with sage and
    avocado 93

Mackerel, lemon and mustard
  67
Magnesium 139
Marinated kipper fillets 19
Marmalade, storing 143
Marrow:
  using leftovers 151

Mayonnaise 152
Meat *see* Beef; Lamb *etc.*
  freezing 147, 148
  storing 144,145
  storing canned 143
  storing cooked 144, 145
Microwave cookers 131
Milk, storing 145
Minerals 138–9
Mixers, food 134
Moules marinière 16
Multi-cookers 131
Mushrooms:
  Baked egg with mushrooms 30
  Lettuce and mushroom cocotte 26
Mussels:
  Moules marinière 16

Neapolitan tomato sauce 153
Noodles:
  Crab noodle soup 9

Offal:
  freezing 147
  storing 145
  Calf's liver with sage and avocado 93
Omelettes:
  Omelette niçoise 31
  Sweet soufflé omelette 109
Onions:
  Potato, carrot and onion casserole 95
Ovens *see* Cookers
Oyster sauce 55

Pan-grilled chicken breasts with herbs 63
Parsley sauce 153
Partridge, traditional roast 90
Pasta:
  calculating quantities 156
  cooking 157
  Basic egg pasta 156
  Fettuccine in creamy ham and mushroom sauce 73
  Tagliatelle with anchovies 20
  Wholemeal pasta 156
Pastry:
  Quick flaky pastry 155
  Shortcrust pastry 154
  Wholemeal pastry 154
Pâté:
  storing 145
  Smoked salmon and cream cheese pâté 17
Peking duck with pancakes 89
Peppers:
  using leftovers 151
  Chakchouka 100
Phosphorus 139
Pitta bread:
  Hot pitta packet 44
Pizza:
  Basic pizza dough 158
  Pizza marinara 71
  Quick pizza dough 158
  Wholemeal pizza dough 158
Plum croûte 121
Plum puddings, individual 118
Poached trout with fennel 76

Pork:
  storing 145
  using leftovers 151
  Hot and sour soup 10
  Pork brochettes 59
  Spiced Indonesian pork 83
Potassium, sources of 139
Potatoes:
  Cheesy salami gratin 45
  Potato, carrot and onion casserole 95
  Swiss fried potatoes 104
Poultry *see* Chicken; Turkey
  freezing 147, 148
  storing 144, 145
Poussins with cream and grapes 86
Prawns:
  Spicy prawn risotto 70
Protein 136–7
Pumpkin:
  using leftovers 151

Radishes:
  Japanese salad 106
Raspberry cheesecakes 117
Refrigerators:
  choosing 132
  cleaning 144
  food storage times 145
Rice, storing 142–3
Risotto, spicy prawn 70
Rolls, quick wholemeal 155
Roquefort rumpburger 53

Sabayon 110
Salad:
  storing 144, 145
  Japanese salad 106
  Wilted salad 107
Salami:
  Cheesy salami gratin 45
  French bread pizza 39
Salmon:
  Buttered salmon steaks 75
  Smoked salmon and cream cheese pâté 17
Sandwiches:
  Bacon, lettuce and tomato toasted sandwich 42
  Californian club sandwich 42
  Croque monsieur 36
Sauce:
  Béarnaise sauce 153
  Bolognese sauce 157
  Cheese sauce 153
  Coating sauce 153
  Hollandaise sauce 152
  Oyster sauce 55
  Parsley sauce 153
  Tomato sauce, Neapolitan 153
  Tomato sauce, simple 153
  White sauce 153
Saucepans 134
Sausages:
  storing 145
  Glazed spicy sausages 47
  Spicy sausages with lentils 60
Sauté of lamb with courgettes and mushrooms 50

Scallops:
  Skewered scallops with bacon 79
Sesame oil (in dressings) 152
Shellfish:
  Crab noodle soup 9
  Moules marinière 16
  Skewered scallops with bacon 79
  Spicy prawn risotto 70
Shortbread fingers 128
Shortcrust pastry 154
Skewered scallops with bacon 79
Slimming diets 139–40
Slow cookers 131–2
Smoked haddock scramble 35
Smoked salmon and cream cheese pâté 17
Snacks:
  Bacon, cheese and apple smokies 41
  Bacon, lettuce and tomato toasted sandwich 42
  Baked egg with mushrooms 30
  Californian club sandwich 42
  Cheesy salami gratin 45
  Croque monsieur 36
  Egg and spinach croûte 32
  Egg Benedict 29
  French bread pizza 39
  Glazed spicy sausages 47
  Hot pitta packet 44
  Omelette niçoise 31
  Smoked haddock scramble 35
  Welsh rarebit 38
Sodium 139
Soufflé, hot chocolate 113
Souffléed cauliflower 96
Soup:
  Asparagus soup 13
  Chilled apple and avocado soup 14
  Crab noodle soup 9
  Ham chowder 13
  Hot and sour soup 10
Spiced Indonesian pork 83
Spicy prawn risotto 70
Spicy sausages with lentils 60
Spinach:
  Egg and spinach croûte 32
  Japanese salad 106
Starters (*see also* Soup):
  Carrot and celeriac vinaigrette 24
  Lettuce and mushroom cocotte 26
  Marinated kipper fillets 19
  Moules marinière 16
  Smoked salmon and cream cheese pâté 17
  Stuffed globe artichoke 23
  Tagliatelle with anchovies 20
  Tapénade 25
Storecupboards, stocking 142–3
Stuffed globe artichokes 23
Sulphur 139
Sunflower oil (in dressings) 152
Swiss fried potatoes 104

Tagliatelle:
  making 156, 157
  Tagliatelle with anchovies 20
Tangerine brûlées 114
Tapénade 25
Tarragon vinegar (in dressings) 152
Thyme vinegar (in dressings) 152
Thiamin 138
Toasters 135
Tofu 10
  Hot and sour soup 10
Tomato sauce:
  Neapolitan 153
  Simple 153
Trout:
  Poached trout with fennel 76
Tuna:
  Pizza marinara 71
  Tapénade 25
Turkey Kiev 64

Veal:
  Escalopes de veau flambé 85
Vegetables:
  freezing 147–8
  storing 145
  using leftovers 151
  Chakchouka 100
Vegetarian diets 141
Vinaigrette, basic 152
Vinegars, herb (in dressings) 152
Vitamins 137–8

Walnut oil (in dressings) 152
Waste disposal 133
Water chestnuts, French beans with 103
Welsh rarebit 38
White sauce, basic 153
Whiting in soured cream with tomatoes 68
Wholemeal pastry 154
  Wholemeal pizza dough 158
  Wholemeal rolls, quick 155
Wilted salad 107
Wines, cooking 143

Yeast, fresh:
  storing 145

Zinc, main sources of 139